W9-ATZ-186

FAITH,
THE YES
OF THE
HEART

Lillian Simons
P.O. Box 65972
Los Angeles CA 90065-0972

FAITH, THE YES OF THE HEART

GRACE ADOLPHSEN BRAME

Augsburg
MINNEAPOLIS

FAITH
The Yes of the Heart

Copyright © 1999 Grace Adolphsen Brame. All rights reserved.

Except for brief quotations in critical articles or reviews, no part of this book may be reproduced in any manner without prior written permission from the publisher. Write to: Permissions, Augsburg Fortress, Box 1209, Minneapolis, MN 55440.

Unless otherwise noted, all Scripture passages are from the New Revised Standard Version of the Bible, copyright © 1946, 1952, 1971 by the Division of Christian Education of the National Council of the Churches of Christ in the U.S.A. Used by permission.

Scripture passages marked KJV are from the King James Version of the Bible.

Iona chant "Take, O take me as I am" appearing page 79 is copyright © Iona Community, admin. GIA Publications. Used by permission.

Excerpted material by Barbara Brown Taylor page 150 is copyright © 1995 Barbara Brown Taylor. All rights reserved. Reprinted by permission from *Gospel Medicine*, published by Cowley Publications, 28 Temple Place, Boston, MA 02111; www.cowley.org (1-800-225-1534).

Cover image © copyright 1999 PhotoDisc. Used by permission.
Cover design by Derek Herzog
Book design by Timothy W. Larson

Library of Congress Cataloging-in-Publication Data
Brame, Grace Adolphsen.
    Faith, the yes of the heart / Grace Adolphsen Brame.
        p. cm.
    Includes bibliographical references and index.
    ISBN 0-8066-3805-2 (alk. paper)
        1. Christian life—Lutheran authors. 2. Luther, Martin, 1483–1546. 3. Faith. I. Title.

BV4501.2.B6856 1999
248.4'841—dc21   99-044990

The paper used in this publication meets the minimum requirements of American National Standard for Information Sciences—Permanence of Paper for Printed Library Materials, ANSI Z329.48-1984.

Manufactured in the U.S.A.   AF 9-3805

03   02   01   00   99   1   2   3   4   5   6   7   8   9   10

To my parents,
Keturah Kepple Adolphsen
and Pastor W. Frederick Adolphsen,
to whom I shall be grateful all my life
for showing me what
commitment and love for God
can be;
to Ed, my husband,
whose generous, affirmative love
has given me freedom to fly
and strength to keep going;
and
to my dear friend Bengt R. Hoffman,
formerly
of Gettysburg Lutheran Theological Seminary,
whose groundbreaking work
on Luther's spirituality
has opened new doors of knowledge.

CONTENTS

ACKNOWLEDGMENTS

My deep gratitude goes to those whose guidance and counsel have meant so much to this book: Professor Gerard S. Sloyan, my mentor and friend; Professor Eric C. Gritsch, Luther Scholar; as well as friends and readers: Dr. Bruce Heggen, Ms. Ruth Ann Loynd, Dr. Ruth Flexman, Dr. Gordon Turk, and Ms. Sue Zorn. I want to acknowledge the scholarly advice of Professor Robert Bornemann, the library staff at the Lutheran Theological Seminary in Philadelphia, and Pastor Richard Lambert of the library at Concordia Theological Seminary, Fort Wayne. The professional expertise of Professor Thomas McDaniel of Eastern Baptist Seminary and Professor James McDonough of St. Joseph's College has been gratefully received. A special note of thanks goes to the staff of the Wilmington Institute Library: Mr. Ben Prestiani, Mr. Thomas Morabito, Ms. Jean Kaufman, and Ms. Chris Paolini. They, along with Professor Sloyan, have gone beyond generosity and have been of inestimable value to me.

Sincerest thanks to my editor, Ron Klug, for asking me to write this book. Thanks to Ron as well for his warmth and patience, his critical eye, and his respect for my own sense of mission. My gratitude also goes to Henry French, editorial director at Augsburg Fortress, for our cordial, rich talks about theology and spirituality. Thanksgivings also to Barbara Owen for her book, *Daily Readings from Luther's Writings* (Augsburg), which alerted me to readings I would have otherwise missed.

I am indebted to my typist, Ms. Linda Flint, and to Drs. Alwin Milian and Carl Gumerman who solved more computer problems than I care to remember. I am grateful to the congregation of Holy Trinity Lutheran Church, where I serve in pastoral capacity, for its understanding and support. Most of all, I am thankful for my husband Ed's incredible understanding and continual affirmation.

*Faith is the yes of the heart, . . .
a confidence on which one stakes one's life.*[1]

—Martin Luther

INTRODUCTION

To be truly alive is to be able to respond. Everything that lives both receives and gives, breathes in and breathes out. To cease to breathe, to respond, is to cease to live. We are alive by the breath of God. It is that life that energizes us, and it is that life that is the only gift we can give away. It is given for us, and it is given for us to give again. It is the Creator's way.

To be fully alive is to be empowered to say yes to the one who created us. The yes we say to God is the yes we say to the life God has given. It comes from the most fundamental level of our being, the level that Jesus and Luther and people across many cultures have called "the heart." Luther called that response "the faith of the heart" or trust,[1] and the quote on which the book's title is based explains it. It is faith as trust that is discussed in the following pages, and Luther's comments about trust, along with those of many others, will be found throughout.

Luther discovered such a trust when his own heart was changed and he claimed he was "reborn."[2] All he *knew about* God and all he had *done for* God became secondary on that day in the tower when the gracious presence of God touched him, embraced him, forgave him, and called him. Those moments were his healing. It was then that he learned what grace truly was, because it encountered and engaged him. That was a dynamic, living experience—not just a thought and not just a piece of information about God. Then he understood something that God had been saying for a very long time: "The righteous . . . live by faith" (Habakkuk 2:4; Romans 1:17). And he understood it at a deeper level than he had ever comprehended it before. He answered, "Yes." And he tried to live out that yes for the rest of his life.

God's loving grace calls forth our yes as well. That yes comes in many forms, all of them called "faith." Faith is far more than a series of statements that can be put into a creed, far more than the result of brilliant theological argument, and far more than a list of answers to life's great questions. It is more than treasured tradition. And it is more than living by the Ten Commandments or the Golden Rule.

Were we to list those approaches that people call "faith," we would have at least five. There is trust or "the faith of the heart, and reasoned belief or theology, which we might call "the faith of the head." There is "the faith of the lips" expressed in confessing our creed or witnessing to others. "The faith we live" is obviously our way of life, and our religious tradition is "the way of faith followed in community."

Faith is not just a matter of understanding God, but of experiencing the real presence of the holy. It is not just a matter of saying what we believe, but of living what we believe, practicing what we preach. Faith is the mortar that binds us to others who have made a covenant with the same creator and parent. Faith is what empowers us to dare to share what matters most with others who are searching for meaning and purpose in their lives.

Faith is the conduit for God's life-giving love. It is not faith that saves us, but God's incredible grace. But grace needs a way to be incarnate. It needs people, lives. It needs a word that can be heard and lips that will speak it. It needs nature to manifest it and sacraments to share it. It needs songs sung and silence in which to listen. Faith receives the love that saves.

Faith that is the experience of God's presence, which trusts in God because it is certain it can depend upon God, is what Luther called "the yes of the heart." It is a personal and interpersonal relationship with the transcendent Holy One. All the Reformers distinguished it from faith that is the result of reasoning, a more objective, impersonal, theological understanding of God and life.

Academically, Luther was trained, like most of us, as a linear thinker, employing hierarchical and "either-or" thought rather than the more inclusive "both-and" approach, which is increasingly used today. His linear thought intensified in debate, and when he was excommunicated from the church in 1521, his polemical work increased. But polemics have never been known to integrate or include both sides of a question. And argument often becomes a matter not just of substance, but of survival. Caught up in those arguments, we too have missed or forgotten many of Luther's compensating thoughts that he voiced at other times.

Luther's followers did not always interpret him well. They naturally followed the custom of the day to "take sides" in arguments rather than to discuss in dialogue as some of us are earnestly trying to do today. The results of the former tendency can be that both sides veer to extremes rather than cooperate in a holistic and integrated response.

In addition, one's followers may take what they wish from a teacher's message and omit aspects that are important. Within a few decades after Luther died, Lutheran theology moved in a direction that ignored or slighted much of Luther's spirituality, his personal, experiential relationship with God. This has made a critical difference in how we perceive him.

Luther was vehemently opposed to scholasticism as he knew and understood it. He considered it to overuse reason as the basis of faith and to underemphasize revelation and trust. Yet thirty years after he died, Lutheran orthodoxy had emerged. According to many contemporary scholars, it was the beginning of a second scholasticism, this time in Protestant form.[3]

Consequently, most of us have learned more of Luther's "theology of the head" than his "theology of the heart." We have analyzed his theological arguments thoroughly, but we have paid little attention to his spirituality, his personal relationship with God, his "faith of the heart." Were we to do that, as we attempt to do here, we would fill a real need.

An example of such need is found in the experience of a pastor, the Reverend Tom Williamson, who speaks of beginning a mission congregation. "I went from house-to-house for months," he said, "not just inviting people to church, but asking what we could do for them. Not one person asked me to explain justification by faith! But many said: 'Is there really a God? If so, can you teach me to know God? Can you teach me to pray?'"[4]

Because of all this and more, we will speak of the forgotten side of Luther, quoting statements that have received little or no attention, words that can give life and hope. As a Lutheran, an academic, a pastoral leader, and retreat leader, I yearn to have people discover more of the unknown Luther. But he should not be presented without comparisons. The subjects we will discuss are enriched, broadened, and strengthened by the thoughts of many others from over the centuries. My own theology of spirituality is basic to the book.

The sentence from which the book's title comes is one of Luther's almost unknown statements. It provides a perfect basis to discuss the integration of theology and spirituality, an approach that has been desperately needed since scholasticism took over philosophy and theology in the twelfth century. Elsewhere I have called this integrated approach a "theology of spirituality."[5] Like the theology of the early church, it begins with study of the Bible in an attitude of prayer. (See, especially, chapter 4.)

Here we will discuss some of the most fundamental and age-old questions: Why was I created? Does God really love me? Can I love God? Can my estrangement from God and others be healed?

We will also speak to some sensitive questions: Is my faith really mine? Has God called me? How do I make the important choices in life? Where is God when I suffer?

Further on we will confront critical but potentially fulfilling challenges: How can I trust in the midst of struggle? Whom or what do I fundamentally love and trust? Is there any hope that you or I can ever change, can ever be closer to the heart of God? Can God, through us, through me, continue to *give life*? Can I stake my life on God?

May the pages ahead clarify, inform, and integrate. More important, may they sustain and give hope.

FAITH: SAYING YES FROM THE HEART

WHEN FAITH IS TRUST

"Faith is the yes of the heart, a confidence on which one stakes one's life." All of Martin Luther's mature life is summed up in this statement spoken in a sermon he delivered six years before he died. I wonder if, when we have finished this book, we will think Luther speaks for us as well.

In just one sentence, Luther summarizes the life of faith. He tells us that faith is primarily living trust in a faithful God, a God to whom we can say yes by the wondrous power of grace. That yes is said not by our lips alone, but by the heart, the deepest part of us. Yet we recognize that in living out our affirmation, we may even risk our lives.

With few words, Luther shares with us his own vibrant and life-giving experience of trust. Perhaps because he knew his weaknesses so well, his dependence on God became stronger. The trust of which he speaks here is a positive, open-faced confidence, affirming God's power in us in spite of all that happens to us.

In 1535, writing on Galatians 2:16, Luther said, "Christian faith is not an empty husk in the heart. . . . If it is true faith, it is a sure trust and firm acceptance in the heart. Christ is . . . present in the faith itself."

Unless Christ is within us, it is impossible to trust, says Luther. Of course we cannot see him, but "Faith . . . is trust in a thing we do not see, in Christ who is present especially when He cannot be seen." There is no confidence unless Christ "lives in the heart."[1]

Luther had been saying this sort of thing for many years. In 1522, when writing his preface to Romans, Luther had made one of his strongest statements on faith: "Faith is a living and unshakable confidence, a belief in the grace of God so assured that a man would die a thousand deaths for its sake."[2]

Such faith is first of all a condition of the heart, a response to God's call of love, and a commitment toward the one on whom we ultimately depend. It is our "Yes!" to the one who matters more than anyone else. It is our side of the most critical relationship we will ever know. It is personal and alive.

Trust is often broken in the world as we know it, but there is one trust that is constantly valid, because the one who gives it is God.

GOD CAN BE TRUSTED

God is always there for us. Faith is the response of being there for God, when the heart is open and the will is given back to God for God to use in love. That is why faith and new life cannot be separated. To give God back the life that has been given, the life that actually belongs to God, is of the essence of faith. But none of us would offer so much unless we believed we could utterly trust the one to whom our lives were given.

The Bible makes clear that God wills our life, our health, and our wholeness, that God forgives and frees. That is what salvation is! And that is the heart of justification: God's forgiving, freeing, healing love!

Yet Scripture can confuse us. Deuteronomy 32:39 announces for God, "I kill and I make alive; I wound and I heal." Many other passages are equally enigmatic.[3] There are people wanting to trust who lose heart as they read such words, wondering if God is fickle or faithful, even wondering if God exists.

Still, as we move through the Bible, we pass through many understandings of God. Yahweh, the God of Israel, is, in Israel's early days, one god "before" all others, but later is known as the only God. Yahweh is first seen as a God of war, of vengeance, but through the later prophets, God asks not for destruction of Israel's enemies, but for justice and mercy. Then through Christ, God asks for far more: for "turning the other cheek," even for prayer for those who stand against us.

Did God change? Surely not. But human understanding of God certainly grew as it moved toward the fullness of time in Christ.

It becomes obvious that the overwhelming message of the Bible is of healing and hope and overflowing life! In Isaiah 42:3, a tender God says of the servant anointed by the Holy Spirit, "A bruised reed he will not break, and a dimly burning wick he will not quench." And Psalm 103 absolutely exults!

> Bless the Lord, O my soul,
> and all that is within me,
> bless his holy name.
> Bless the Lord, O my soul,
> and do not forget all his benefits—
>   who forgives all your iniquity,
> who heals all your diseases,
> who redeems your life from the Pit,
> who crowns you with steadfast love and mercy,
>   who satisfies you with good as long as you live
> so that your youth is renewed like the eagle's.
> . . . Bless the Lord, O my soul!

In Isaiah 43:2 we read, "When you pass through the waters, I will be with you; . . . when you walk through fire, you shall not be burned." Look ahead! cries Isaiah 35:4-5, God "will come and save you. Then the eyes of the blind shall be opened, and the ears of the deaf unstopped." Following the latter Isaiah comes Ezekiel, who, in a vision, sees a field filled with bones of the dead, bones that come to life by the awesome power of the Holy Spirit (Ezekiel 37).

About six hundred years later, Jesus' voice is heard announcing, "I came that they may have life . . . abundantly" (John 10:10). "I am the resurrection and the life. Those who believe in me, even though they die, will live" (11:25). The very heart of Jesus' mission is revealed in his words in the synagogue at Nazareth (Luke 4:18-19), words that Isaiah had said so long before:

> The Spirit of the Lord is upon me,
> because he has anointed me to bring good news to the poor.
> He has sent me to proclaim release to the captives
> and recovery of sight to the blind,
> to let the oppressed go free,
> to proclaim the year of the Lord's favor.

"The year of the Lord" was the jubilee year, coming every fifty years, when all debts and sins were supposed to be forgiven and grace was intended to reign throughout the land.

Jesus defined God as Spirit to the woman at the well. In John 4:24, Jesus said, "God is Spirit," clearly and directly, cutting through mountains of theological arguments that would define God. As John 6:63 says, "It is the spirit that gives life." Thus the Nicene Creed proclaims the Spirit as "the Lord and giver of life."

Every aspect of God, as creator, redeemer, and inspirer, includes the dynamic action of creating and recreating life. This is the overwhelming biblical message. If God exists at all, God exists as lifegiver. The first and last words of God are words of life!

God is what God says. God's words reveal God's being. Surely, in the initial moments of creation, God was what God is now. If we put all of God's commands into one sentence, we would hear what God is always saying: "Let there be life!" God, then and now, calls all things, including us, to life!

What God did by speaking those words, God will always do. And what God was for us then, as life-giver, God will always be. On that we can depend. Because of that, we can hope.

We cannot live if we have no hope. And we cannot hope if we have no faith in something or someone on whom we can depend, someone to whom, with all our hearts, we can answer, "Yes!"

Answering "Yes"

Yes is perhaps the most powerful word in the world. It is a word of life when it creates, builds, and heals. It is a word of death when it assents to that which deforms, misleads, and destroys the goodness of relationships or the potential of a soul.

Saying yes may have far-reaching consequences. We may say yes to someone with whom we intend to live all our life or yes to creating the life of a child or yes to a major turn in the road of life. Sometimes we must say yes to releasing precious, but lesser, loves for one that matters most of all. And conversely, we may say yes to hopelessness and despair. In every case, we have made a decision that will deeply affect and even define our lives and also the lives of others.

What then of our choices toward God? Can we love God? Can we offer our lives to God? Can we say yes to God? There are theologians who say that our flawed human nature makes that impossible. But God asks for our love, asks for our yes, even commands it. The *Shema*, the ancient creed of Israel, contains the beginning of the Great Commandment given by Jesus. Mark's version reads, "You shall love the Lord your God with all your heart, and with all your soul, and with all your mind, and with all your strength" (12:30). It is impossible to have a more complete or comprehensive command (see chapter 4).

There is more. God not only commands but covenants with us. Covenants exist only through cooperation, a cooperation made possible solely through God's power given to us. We are responsible and response-able to cover our part of the agreement.

A covenant is far more than an agreement. It is a mutual promise, a binding pledge, a vow usually taken with an oath and meant to be lasting. A covenant says for each participant, "I will be there for you, and I will depend that you will be there for me." According to Luther, we can say yes to God only by God's grace. Luther writes, "This faith does not grow by our own powers. On the contrary, the Holy Spirit is present and writes it in the heart."[4] For me that means we can say yes to God because God gives us the will, the strength, the grace to do so. Paul said the same thing in Philippians 2:13: "For it is God who is at work in you, enabling you both to will and to work for his good pleasure." Despair is not our only choice. There is hope!

Evelyn Underhill writes in *The Ways of the Spirit* that our ability to say yes or no to God is the most awesome gift we have been given by the creator.[5] Surely, such a gift is the pure grace of God, humbling to us who so often seek for authority and power. It is the grace of a parent who loves us enough to let us answer freely, on our own, to the call of love that is offered.

Faith is God's gift planted in a receptive heart. It is like seed, said Jesus, planted in the ground. Some blows away. Some has no nourishment where it is planted, and some is choked by other things (the negatives of life? too much to do? suffering and pain? choices for less important things?). But sometimes the seed is eagerly received. The heart says yes and begins to soften like the shell of a seed in the soil. Set in the ground of God's being, the energy and warmth of God's love and the water of life, the Spirit, are poured out so that faith may grow. At the same time that the gift of faith is offered, the capacity to receive it must be given, too. Faith and freedom coexist. Faith cannot exist without freedom. Often Luther insisted that God never forces faith on us.[6] This must be true. Were it forced, it would not be ours, and it would not be faith.

Jesus, in his full humanity, knew the consequences of saying yes. "Not my will, but thine be done," he cried out, even as he sweat blood. It was yes for him all the way. It was yes to the one who sent and guided him. It was yes to the cross. It was yes to the resurrection. It was yes as he offered the Holy Spirit to the fear-filled ones who followed him.

For Jesus, Amen truly was yes. It means "to be firm," "to trust in," "to believe," "with certainty," "to be convinced," "to be committed."[7] Our Amen is a yes to God, who, in Christ, has said yes to us (2 Corinthians 1:19, 20).

THE HEART: CENTER OF OUR BEING

One Sunday morning at my home church, the pastor quizzed the congregation. He looked directly at me and said, "How many times do you think the word *heart* is mentioned in the Bible?" I stammered out an answer that was exceedingly short of the mark. Smiling, he responded, "I looked in my concordance and counted *heart* almost nine hundred times!"

Why should that word be so important? Take a moment and think of the first scriptural quotations that come to your mind. For me they were: "Out of the abundance of the heart, the mouth speaks" (Matthew 12:34); "Where your treasure is, there will your heart be also" (Matthew 6:21); "For it is the God who said, 'Let light shine out of darkness,' who has shone in our hearts to give the light of the knowledge of the glory of God in the face of Jesus Christ" (2 Corinthians 4:6). The compelling, telling statements go on and on.

In words to Ezekiel, God promised restoration and renewal to Israel: "I will give them one heart, and put a new spirit within them; I will remove the heart of stone from their flesh and give them a heart of flesh. . . . They shall be my people, and I will be their God" (Ezekiel 11:19-20).

When the word *heart* is used in the scriptures of "the Religions of the Book," it rarely refers to the organ beating in our breasts. Instead it refers to the center, the very core of our whole being: body, mind, and spirit. We all recognize that this is Jesus' point when he speaks of words and actions coming from our hearts. He is saying that who we really are, what we really believe, what we most deeply desire, is hidden in our depths. He is pointing out that this deep level affects how we feel, what we think, and what we decide to do. "Heart" refers to the very root of our desires. It refers to what we truly love. It refers to our will. And it refers to our genuine self, not the persona we present to society. It is the heart that God seeks. And we say it is the heart that we give when we offer our lives to God. We offer the very core, the center of our being: our spirit.

On Sunday mornings, Lutherans sing an offertory using the words of Psalm 51: "Create in me a clean heart, O God, and renew a right spirit within me." Luther explained: "The word 'heart' in German is almost the same as what the Hebrew calls 'spirit.' What in Latin we call 'mind, intellect, will, affections'—almost all this the Germans render as 'heart.'"[8] For writers of Hebrew scripture, the heart was the center of intellect, emotion, will, consciousness, perception, and memory. Through it, human beings awaken and respond to God and others. For the ancient Hebrews, a person of "no heart" had no understanding, and the dead were referred to as "out of heart."[9] Furthermore, the inner spirit or intention of the heart is essential to give meaning to all outer forms, especially in worship and prayer.[10]

To say yes, to say Amen to God is to proclaim: "I believe with all my heart." To say yes from the depths of the heart is to follow God, not merely by words or deeds, but from the center of our being. We "stake our lives" on God with that reply.

WE STAKE OUR LIVES

Luther wrote from experience about staking one's life. He had done it, escaping from his defense at Worms to spend many months hidden from view in Wartburg Castle. He had wanted to purify the church and to inspire it to new understandings and new ways. But he was seen by many to be destroying it. Furthermore, culture, politics, and economics—the very fabric of society—seemed, in the eyes of those who disagreed, to be threatened, not helped. It was not just Luther's reputation but his very life that was on the line. No wonder he could write in his hymn "A Mighty Fortress,"

And though this world with devils filled,
Should threaten to undo us;
We will not fear, for God hath willed
His truth to triumph through us . . .
Let goods and kindred go,
This mortal life also:
The body they may kill:
God's truth abideth still.
His kingdom is forever![11]

As the daughter of missionaries, I personally know that there are those who are willing to "stake their lives" on loving God and telling Jesus' story. In order to minister to his people, my father walked alone through areas where tigers roamed. My parents found a cobra coiled right beside their bed. They offered back to God, at birth, the lives of two long-awaited daughters, born without apt medical attention. Back in this country, I remember waiting prayerfully for my father's return from a counseling session with a man who he thought might kill him. It was something that actually happened to one of our pastor friends.

Neither of my parents ever "sounded a trumpet before them." Instead, they felt themselves unspeakably privileged to do the work they had been given. They had neither Luther's more bombastic personality nor his way with words, but they understood well the meaning of his hymn.

What we live for, we die for. Each moment of living is also a moment of dying. It will never return. We cannot do it over. What we say yes to from the heart is our treasure, whatever it may be. On that, whether we realize it or not, we stake our lives.

Trusting Our Beginning and Our End
(based on John 1:1-5)

In the beginning was Love.
Love was with God,
and God's very being
was the being of Love.
God's being and God's expression were one.

Love was in the beginning with God,
Love, the creative energy,
moving out from itself
in birthing all that is:
matter and all living things.

Without Love was not anything made
that was made.
In this Love was Life,
and that Life was the Light of humankind,
given to glow within them, from them,
given to show the Way.

That revelation endures
in spite of darkness;
That Love endures
in spite of ignorance and pain.
No evil, no lack of knowledge, no suffering
can destroy it.
That Love will always be.

BORN FROM THE HEART OF GOD

"WE LOVE BECAUSE GOD FIRST LOVED US."

We have been loved to life. We were born in the heart of God before we were born on earth. We were cherished by God before we were humanly conceived.

Scripture tells of God's intimate involvement in our beginnings. Counseling a frightened teenage Jeremiah, God reveals: "Before I formed you in the womb I knew you, and before you were born I consecrated you!" (Jeremiah 1:5). Paul writes of the one who "set me apart before I was born . . . and called me through . . . grace" (Galatians 1:15). And Isaiah almost sings: "The Lord called me before I was born, while I was in my mother's womb he named me." Formed in the womb to be God's servant, Israel is commissioned: "You are my servant, Israel, in whom I will be glorified" (Isaiah 49:1, 3).

One of the most compelling messages about God's involvement is in Psalm 139:13-16, which says:

> For it was you who formed my inward parts;
> you knit me together in my mother's womb.
> . . . .
> My frame was not hidden from you,
> when I was being made in secret,
> intricately woven in the depths of the earth.
> Your eyes beheld my unformed substance.
> In your book were written
> all the days that were formed for me,
> when none of them as yet existed.

Thinking about this passage in his *Summaries of the Psalms*, Luther spoke of this poet and singer, who knew that "even in his mother's womb, before he was made, God has been with him."[1]

Deuteronomy 32:18 even speaks of "the God who gave you birth." What a beginning! We could paraphrase the first chapter of John, as above, to say:

> In the beginning was love.
> . . . .
> Love, the creative energy,
> moving out from itself
> in birthing all that is:
> matter and all living things.

A love like this is grace: living, vibrant, energetic grace. How amazing! The one who is so generous and powerful loves us even though we are sometimes so selfish and so small! Yet this is what true parental love is all about. It is passed on to us from God. Why would God love us? We can understand only from our own experience.

Most of us want to have children, or, if we have none, to nurture people, young or old, who need someone to notice them and care. We have a need to give life, to love, to nourish, to uphold: to pass on to another what matters so much to us. This need seems to be part of God's creative force, built into our being. In our own way, we participate in God's work: the holy and awesome process of giving life. Nothing can match that.

If God is love, God is impelled to love. And if God is Life, Being, the eternal "I Am," then God's life must overflow. God must have living things to love.

Love is the most potent force in the world. We live for it. We die for it. We hunger for it. And we die for lack of it. The unseen energy that began and sustains the universe is the energy of love.

WHY DO WE LOVE GOD?

But do we love God? We might adore God because God is wonderful and wise. We might sing praises because God is powerful and pure. We have even been commanded to love God by the writer of Deuteronomy and by Jesus himself, who said that the "greatest and first commandment" is to love God with all our being (Matthew

22:37-38 after Deuteronomy 6:5). But does anyone love because of being commanded to? Who can be forced to love?

Sometimes we are wooed to love by goodness or tenderness or kindness or beauty. Sometimes we are compelled to love by another's need. But we do not love God because we are told to.

We love simply "because God first loved us." God started it. And we can't help but respond. It was God who gave us the capacity to love. It is our greatest and most exciting gift, for, at bottom, it is love that creates life. Love is our most God-like quality. We are most like God when we love. But we rarely love purely.

Luther once wrote a sermon on the first and second commandments as they appear in Matthew 22:35-40. Nothing could be more clear than his words describing how inadequate we are without God. Of loving God with all our hearts, he states: "Human nature *alone* will never be able to accomplish what God in this commandment requires, namely, which we surrender our will to the will of God. *No one* has kept this commandment"[2] (italics added).

The obvious response to Luther, then, is "Why are we commanded to do something none of us can do?" And Luther is ready with the answer: only the Holy Spirit can do it in and through us. The heart is renewed by the Spirit:

> When I believe from the heart that Christ did this for me, I receive also the same Holy Spirit that makes me entirely new. . . . Then . . . I do everything he desires of me; not in my own strength, but by the strength of him that is in me, as Paul says in Philippians 4:13: "I can do all things through Christ [who] strengthens me."[3]

From my point of view, these are two of the most important sentences Luther ever wrote. They explain many of his sayings that otherwise seem to be in opposition to each other, particularly those regarding human nature and divine grace, those regarding the self-centered self and the self given back to God.

In a Pentecost *postil* (a model sermon written for other pastors to give), Luther goes further than he does above. He is convinced that God's love must first soften the heart before we can love back, before we can have faith: "I must first be loved—must first feel the great treasure and blessing in Christ." Here the bombastic Luther is entirely absent. His words are personal, almost confessional: "God takes the very first step and allows his dear child to die for me before I ask him to do so, . . . before I ever know him. Then a confidence and love grow in me."[4]

Most of the saints have told us that we should love God for God's self. With this, too, Luther agreed. Writing about the Magnificat, he says that Mary "teaches us to love and praise God for Himself alone and not selfishly to seek anything at His hands." Luther warns us not to "use" God for the gifts we hope to receive or to seek our own advantage through God's grace. Instead, he asks us to look for "the bare, unfelt goodness that is hidden in God."

His words strike most to the heart when he says that some have "delighted in their salvation much more than in the Savior, in the gift more than the Giver, in the creature rather than in the Creator."[5] Avoiding this is perhaps the greater challenge.

The most shocking realization is that we have sometimes made God into a mere provider, someone who is useful only in giving us what we want but for whom we have no use if that does not happen. God is supposed to be all good, which means that, regardless of our choices and those of others, God is believable only if nice things happen to us. Otherwise God is not love. Why, then, should we love God back?[6]

For a long time I have asked myself why I do not love God as we are told we should. We are taught that we should not love God for what God does for us or even for what God is to us. We should love God for God's own sake. But I do not know how that is possible.

I love God because God loves me, because God has breathed into the matter of earth God's own life and created me and all whom I love and cherish. I love God because I can trust God, because I am told, "Lo, I am with you always, even to the end of the earth." I trust that I will never be abandoned, that I will not walk alone through the valleys nor stand alone in the presence of my enemies.

I love God because God feeds me. I cannot live without God, nor can any living thing. I feed on God. I drink in God and breathe in God.

> Ho, everyone who thirsts! Come to the waters. Even you who have nothing to give, come! You shall receive wine and milk . . . (Author's paraphrase.) Take and eat. This is my body. Take and drink. . . . For my flesh is true food and my blood is true drink.

I love God because God has taught me how to love. I have been loved into loving. In receiving what I have been given, I have also learned how to give it away. This capacity is God's image in me, for "God is love."

In the last analysis, I can never get away from my contingency, my dependence on my creator and parent. God is God, and I am only God's creature and child. I can never love God as much as God loves me. My glory and my strength are God's life, which flows into me and through me. My truest identity cannot be found in fame or accomplishments, personality or possession. My truest identity is found in being a vessel for God's life, a vessel through which God reveals God's self. God is a gift to me. In those special moments when my life is given to the Giver, when it ceases to seem to be my own possession, I can do God's work. Through my surrender, God can offer creative, redeeming, and re-creative love through me.

ESTRANGEMENT

But often it is not that way. In despair, I may find I am not all God created me to be. This is true for all of us. We can easily be estranged from those around us and from their ways of life. In our conflicting loyalties, we are estranged from God and even from our own true selves.

We are lonely. We are lonely because of dissimilarities in opportunity, training, and culture. We are lonely because we are exceptionally gifted or seem ungifted. We are lonely because of what we have or what we lack. We are lonely because of misunderstanding, distrust, rejection, and victimization. We are lonely because we are not noticed, and we are lonely because we haven't looked deeply enough into others to notice what can be brought to life in them.

We are lonely because of our own self-image, because of inadequacy, shame, guilt, or sin. And we are just as lonely because of our inability to accept forgiveness, to forgive another, or even to forgive ourselves. We are lonely in our inner pain and fear. We fear to lose the walls that protect us. Therefore they hedge us in and prevent possibilities from coming true. We cannot receive love that is offered, or we do not even realize it is available. Unaware, we may be facing in the wrong direction, facing away from the Source of love.

Our loneliness doesn't mean God is gone. It means that just as we are unaware of the air we breathe, we are not conscious of the pervasive presence of God. We are absent from God, but God is not absent from us.

The disconnection is from our side, in our experience, our incomprehension—not God's. We are still carved upon God's heart, still held in God's hands.

It is God who keeps the estrangement from being complete. God goes out in search of us as the parable of the lost sheep says. God goes with us even into Sheol, the abode of the dead, as Psalm 139 affirms. It is God's faithful love that keeps the relationship from being severed. Treasured words rise in our memory: "I will never leave you or forsake you" (Hebrews 13:5); "When you pass through the waters, I will be with you" (Isaiah.43:2); "I have called you by name, you are mine" (Isaiah 43:1).

Evelyn Underhill wrote in *The Ways of the Spirit* that nothing can ever change the fact that we are the children of our parents. We always will be, even if we sin against them. It is the same with God.[7] Even if sin breaks the relationship from our side, we are, as Acts 17:28 reminds us, still God's "offspring."

Sin destroys our ability to be free and open in our relationship with God, but it does not destroy God's love. That is probably why the saints remind us that we are distinct from God, meaning "different," but never completely separated.

God is where we are, no matter how good or bad we are, no matter how confused we may be, no matter whether we have the answers we seek. Meister Eckhart, the fourteenth-century Dominican, wrote:

> God is nearer to me than I am to myself. My being depends upon God's intimate presence. So, too, he is nearer to a stick or a stone, but they do not know it. . . . Man is not blessed because God is in him and so near that he has God—but that he is aware of how near God is, and knowing God, he loves him.[8]

Estrangement cannot be the last word. God's kingdom shall come. But I do not believe God will impose it. I believe the kingdom must come in individual hearts until it fills the earth. Isaiah and Habakkuk were bold enough to say, "The earth will be full of the knowledge of the Lord as the waters cover the sea" (Isaiah 11:9; see Habakkuk 2:14).

Human Nature: Impediment and Instrument

Luther struggled with human nature. His own anxiety about his relationship to God was like a deep, recurring illness, destroying his power and his peace. He speaks often of this *Anfechtung*. Like Augustine, he realized keenly the self-centeredness to which every individual is naturally prone: the need to have pleasure, possessions, prestige, and power over others; the obsession to have our own desires fulfilled. He called it "being curved in upon oneself" to such a degree that we replace God in our own hearts.[9] So it was that he wrote the following:

> Nature is so evil that it . . . seeks nothing except itself and its own advantage. In everything it sees, seeks, and has in mind only itself. . . . Nature puts itself in place of everything, even in the place of God, and seeks only that which is its own and not that which is God's. . . . Nature is its own first and greatest idol.[10]

Surely no words could be stronger than these! But they are about human nature that has disconnected itself from God, not human nature as a vessel and instrument of God. And in the latter, Luther believed profoundly (see chapters 3 and 10).

Luther's beloved *Theologia Germanica*, which he published twice in his lifetime, was very clear about this point. It explains that all things are good to the extent that they live in God. Therefore all creation is good, as Genesis 1 says over and over, except when it is separated from God. It states: "There is nothing without God except one thing: to will otherwise than the eternal will. . . . No will should be without my will."[11]

The *Theologia* continues to explain that our wills really belong to God and that when we surrender them they become what they were intended to be. When this happens, we are not divided. Peace comes. The question is no longer whether our decisions are God's will or our own. God's will can become our own. By the grace of the Holy Spirit in us, we can want what God wants. When that happens, God's will shall "be done on earth as in heaven." God's dream for us will not be fulfilled until grace lives in and through our nature, glorifying the one who made it.

Our only hope is that by the winsome power of that Spirit of grace, we who are caught in such self-interest as Luther describes can still feel the power and the pull of God's love for us and say yes to it. This is the discovery of new life and true freedom. This is what Jesus called a "new birth" and the Reformers referred to as "regeneration." This is what Luther was referring to when he said, "I receive . . . the Holy Spirit . . . which makes me entirely new."[12] This is the gift of faith.

Faith is the yielded will, a gift given by the grace of God, a dynamic gift that receives grace as we receive communion: with our whole being.

Would we, after such a rebirth, still will to take God's place in our own hearts? Would we, as children of grace, still stumble? Would we be called again and again to return to the one who gives true life?

Luther would simply answer: "Yes. We will always be both sinful and saved."[13] We will always sin, but we are forgiven, loved, and led. God asks for our trust, our obedience, and our love. But God's life-giving love makes up the difference between what we would be and what we are not.

Again this is parent love, a love that that is faithful in spite of what we do or are, a love that inspires us to do and be what we can do and be. This is the kind of love that, without even thinking, will give its life for us, its children. This is the love of the cross.

There is no cross without cost, but the cost is passed aside. It is worth it, from God's point of view, for the sake of love. If our lack can be filled, our brokenness healed, our hope regained, and life given purpose and meaning, the giver of life will do it over and over again. Our task is to live receiving.

THE ENTICING GOD

God woos to win us but does not compel. God invites and entices but does not force. God loves and leads but does not intervene or manipulate. God inspires but does not control us.

No gift forced upon a receiver is a gift; it is an imposition. It is a demand. Grace is neither. God gives us our freedom but never robs us of it. Our lives, our wills, our hearts are given us so that we can give them back to God.

Luther did not always seem to understand this, but he had many moments when he did. He said more things than we can quote about love that leads rather than compels:

> Christ does not horribly force and drive us. Rather he teaches us in a loving and friendly way. . . . Christ drives and compels no one. Indeed he teaches so gently that he entices rather than commands.[14]

> Faith will not force and press anyone to accept the Gospel: it leaves the matter to the choice of every person.[15]

Luther was sure that confidence in God's grace is the work of the Holy Spirit and that "because of it, without compulsion, a person is ready and glad to do good to everyone."[16]

The same point is movingly made by Henri Nouwen in *The Return of the Prodigal Son*. Speaking of both sons, Nouwen says:

> How much [God] would have liked to pull them back with his fatherly authority and hold them close to himself so that they would not get hurt. . . . But his love is too great to do any of that. It cannot force, constrain, push, or pull. It offers the freedom to reject that love or to love in return. . . . The Father's heart knows all the pain that will come from that choice, but his love makes him powerless to prevent it. . . . He cannot make them love him without losing his true fatherhood.[17]

LIVING IN GOD[18]

God is where we are, even when we do not know where that is. We cannot be lost from God. God, who is more than we can see or know, fathom or explain, is the most pervasive force in the universe. "There is no hole in God!" my wonderful physician once exclaimed. The God whom we describe as omnipresent really is!

Born in the heart of God, we have never left that presence, for it has always surrounded us, filling the heavens and the earth. It becomes a living presence when we truly hear the words of the Bible and when we truly see God acting. Acts 17:28 declares, "In him we live and move and have our being." Jesus says in John 15:4, "Abide in me as I abide in you." Paul testifies in Ephesians 4:4-6: "There is one God and Father of us all, who is above all and through all and in all."

Hildegard of Bingen is inspired to say in simple terms: "God hugs you. You are encircled by the arms of the mystery of God."[19] And well known Norwegian Lutheran theologian Olé Hallesby writes in *Prayer*:

> The air which our souls need . . . envelopes all of us at all times and on all sides. God is round about us in Christ on every hand, with his many-sided and all-sufficient grace. All we need to do is to open our hearts.[20]

The theme is pervasive among many inspired writers. Evelyn Underhill notes that barometric pressure exerts some force every moment of our lives but is so constant that we do not realize its presence. So too is the presence of God.

In *The Double Search*, Rufus Jones, the well-known Quaker professor of philosophy, writes of God who "enfolds and enwreathes the finite spirit" as the ocean and the sun surround living things. Jones points out something of great importance: in the world of nature, living things are surrounded, touched, and penetrated by sun and water because they have no will. Among human beings, God "can be received only through appreciation and conscious appropriation." Jones adds, "He comes only through doors that are *purposely* open for him."[21]

With that purposeful intention Luther once prayed:

> O heavenly Father, give us our daily bread so that Christ may remain in us eternally and we in him.[22]

When he felt this way, Luther knew peace. Lecturing on Galatians 2:19-20, he commented simply: "Since I am in him, no evil can befall me." This was the state in which trust was possible for him and the anxiety from which he often suffered passed away.[23]

It is this sense of peace and bubbling joy that is at the heart of the marvelous spiritual "He's Got the Whole World in His Hands." All of my concerts in the former communist Soviet Union in the 1980s ended with that spiritual. I sang it to share with those people, who were supposed to be my enemies, the sure love of God that reaches out to enfold us all.

The first time I sang the spiritual was during a concert at an off-limits institute where some of the most sensitive space research was being carried on. I had no idea how the song would be received, and I realized that I could be putting myself in danger because it was a statement of faith. But after five curtain calls and a repetition of the spiritual, I got the message: we could sing what we could not say, and it meant everything! So I sang: "He's got the whole world in his hands. . . . He's got the sun and the moon, . . . the wind and the rain, . . . the gamblin' man, . . . the itsy-bitsy baby, . . . you and me, . . . *everybody here right in his hands.* He's got the whole world in his hands!"

As I sang and they listened, there were those present who knew we were at home in our birthplace, in the place where we all belonged, in the very heart of God. There we were related by birth. In those moments, we remembered and realized it was true.

In one sense, you, I, none of us, have ever left the place where we began. Although we may no longer be aware of it, God wondrously watches over us. Now and forever, we live within the heart of God, enfolded and upheld:

> I am convinced that neither death, nor life, nor angels, nor rulers, nor things present, nor things to come, nor powers, nor height, nor depth, nor anything else in all creation, will be able to separate us from the love of God in Christ Jesus our Lord. (Romans 8:38-39)

CHRIST BORN IN
THE HUMAN HEART

"Be Born in Us Today"

No matter how often we sing them, the simple words and music of Phillips Brooks's "O Little Town of Bethlehem" transport us to that night in which the Christ child came to earth. Through a gentle, quiet tune and pictures made by words, we enter the time and place when God, transcendent and unfathomable, was born into human history—in a human way, in terms a human being could best understand.

As the carol proceeds, our words become a prayer. It is a prayer that asks for something incredible: that the miracle be reproduced, and that this time, the event not simply happen in history, but in us.

> How silently, how silently
> The wondrous gift is given!
> So God imparts to human hearts
> The blessings of his heav'n.
> No ear may hear his coming;
> But in this world of sin,
> Where meek souls will receive him, still
> The dear Christ enters in.
>
> O Holy Child of Bethlehem,
> Descend to us, we pray.
> Cast out our sin, and enter in,
> Be born in us today.[1]

Other carols breathe the same prayer. One, at first lamenting that Christ came to earth to "find no room," eagerly and repeatedly responds:

O come to my heart, Lord Jesus:
There is room in my heart for thee.[2]

The implications of what happened that night in Bethlehem reach throughout all the centuries that have followed, affecting the inside and outside of history. We count time from what was long thought to be the year of that happening. In that human sense alone, it is the most outstanding of all events.

Whole societies have been influenced by that birth. So have their customs, their art, their learning, and the way people care for each other. But none of this would have happened had not the hearts of individuals, both famous and unknown, been touched and transformed first.

Angelus Silesius, a seventeenth-century poet, commented, "Though Christ a thousand times be born, if he's not born in you, your heart's forlorn."[3] If the birth of Christ does not happen to us personally, we are still lost, alone, and estranged. Nothing changes in you or in me or in our world unless that birth happens inside us, in the very center of our beings:

> Inside—in our hearts, where we are grasped most deeply by what matters.
>
> Inside—where what we feel is translated into what we do.
>
> Inside—where every moment we decide what to live for and how.
>
> Inside—where Luther says we are taught by God.[4]

LUTHER'S "CHILD OF THE HEART"

Through the centuries, many have written of the human heart as the intended birthplace of the Christ. Luther is quoted as having said in a Christmas sermon of 1520:

> This Child is sent to fill thine heart,
>   and for no other reason is he born.
> No word can say nor understand
>   how so small a thing
>   should hold so great a treasure.
> Thus the great and wonderful sign is repeated,
>   and the heart is made sweet and glad and
>   fearless,

for it is at peace
with all the suffering that may befall it,
for what should cause it woe?
Where the Child is, all will be well.
The heart and the Child cannot be parted.[5]

Then, in 1534 or 1535, Luther wrote a Christmas hymn for his children. The hymn, "From Heaven Above" included the lines:

O dear Lord Jesus, for your head,
Now I will make the softest bed.
The chamber where this bed shall be
Is in my heart, inside of me.[6]

Perhaps the person best known for speaking about Christ born in human hearts is Meister Eckhart (1260–1328), who built upon the thoughts of many who had preceded him.[7] It was he who influenced another Dominican, Johannes Tauler (1261–1306), and it was Johannes Tauler whom Luther considered his greatest teacher.

Preaching on Christmas Day, Eckhart refers to "the One who . . . is born today, within time, in human nature," and then says, "St. Augustine says that this birth is always happening. And yet, if it does not occur in me, how could it help me? Everything depends on that." That birth, says Eckhart, is the Word speaking to the soul—in "its purest element," in its core, its essence. There in the "central silence" of the creature, where we are most simple, no ideas are present. We are passive. God alone has access. God alone acts. In that silence, the word of God can be heard, and when it is heard, it is born in us.[8]

It is understandable that Luther would have appreciated this approach to the birth of Christ, passed on through Tauler. For Luther, as Paul had said so clearly, "Faith comes from what is heard, and what is heard comes through the word of Christ" (Romans 10:17).

But what does Christ in my heart have to do with Christ in history? Jesus was not known outside his tiny homeland until after he died, rose, and ascended. He conquered no armies. He wrote no books to preserve his message. He built no monuments as reminders of his mission. He was not a financial, political, or artistic success. He had no possessions and wielded no earthly power. But he changed people's hearts, and through them, he changed history.

Luther pointed out that even the devil believes that Christ was born, but the devil has never had the personal experience of faith. For the devil, that means that the birth of Jesus is only a fact of history as "even heretics" confess. It surely is not trust and commitment: depending on God and committing one's life to God's will and way.[9]

Luther wrote that if we truly observe Christmas, "Christ [will] be formed in us. It is not enough that we should hear his story if the heart be closed. I must listen, not to a history, but to a gift."[10] For Luther, "listening to a gift" meant to receive it not only through the ears but in the heart.

Since faith comes by hearing, the gospel must be proclaimed aloud, but the meaning of its message must also be heard. The Holy Spirit preaches. The Spirit speaks through sound and silence, with words and wordlessly. To hear simply with the ears is not the same as receptive listening. The heart's receptivity is vitally important.[11]

Luther urges us to hear the glorious, life-giving words of the angels as though they were spoken to each of us personally and individually. "To you is born a Saviour!" (Luke 2:11)[12]

"To me?" I ask. "Yes, to me!" When those words are finally planted in my heart, I have heard the gospel.

In a Christmas sermon from 1530, Luther lays his heart before Mary with a simple surrender to her child: "I know none, neither humans nor angels, who can help me except this child whom you, O Mary, hold in your arms."[13] Thus he again explains reasonable, historical faith as well as the receptivity that is the faith of the heart, calling them this time "the two kinds of faith." He longs for his people to know the latter.

Luther's seal may well come to mind. There Christ, represented by the cross, is set in the center of Luther's own heart.[14] Well might that insignia say for each of us, "Christ is my treasure. He gives himself to me at the very center of my being. I offer my open heart to be 'branded by his cross.'" Paul had said: "Jesus Christ has made me his own." And Luther could have replied to that text, as he suggested elsewhere, "And I have made him mine."

An old, cherished Scandinavian hymn seems to say what Luther's insignia does:

> On my heart imprint your image,
> Blessed Jesus, king of grace,

That no riches, cares, or pleasures
Has the power you to efface.
This the superscription be:
"Jesus crucified for me
Is my life, my sure foundation,
And my glory and salvation."[15]

Luther's "yes of the heart" is such a confidence in Christ, a confidence that can "not grow by our own powers." Rather, it is a security that comes only by one means: "the Holy Spirit is present and writes it in the heart."[16]

GOD'S LIFE IN US

There is perhaps no more persistent theme in the long story of spirituality than that of God's asking entrance into the heart. "Listen! I am standing at the door, knocking; if you hear my voice and open the door, I will come into you and eat with you, and you with me," says Revelation 3:20. The metaphor of the door has consistently been interpreted by theologians and artists as referring to the human heart.[17] And the New Testament has numerous references to the coming of the Holy Spirit to us, among us, and into us; of Christ's life as our life, and of God within.

Traditional Christian spirituality sees each of these as a way of saying that God's life and presence are shared with us on the deepest and most personal level. This is the level at which human beings experience that God is real and God is love. It is the level at which repentance, conversion, and commitment begin. It is the root level of transformation of life.

Traditional Christian spirituality responds to this outpouring, this *kenosis*, this self-giving of God, by learning to receive this life and love. But many movements today confuse receiving God into the center of our lives with the human tendency to see ourselves as the center of life.

Christ's birth, God's life, never becomes our possession, but we can become its instruments. The creature can never control the creator. We can only allow God to use us more completely. This is not an occasion for spiritual pride, but one of awe, joy, and willingness to be led. The birth of Christ within us is the only way God has provided for the work of the incarnation to be continued.

Having God's life within us does not mean that each of us has "a piece" or "a part" of God inside. It does not mean that if we put all of us together, we would have God or that God is merely a force of nature capable of its own fulfillment. It surely does not mean that we become God and therefore replace God. Nor does it mean that we are the same as God, acting as though there is more than one divinity, making all of us rivals of the one true God.

It *does* mean, however, that God is not just an idea, someone we have concocted to explain life and to motivate us. It does mean that God is more than an impersonal force that rules the world from above and outside. It means that God's presence is available at the deepest levels of our being, that God cares about us personally and individually from the inside out. And it means that God has gotten to our core.

WHEN THE HEART SAYS "YES"

Christ born in us is more than a romantic notion or poetic talk. Asking God to be born in us is inviting the life that is greater than our own to take command, to reign in us. It is not just saying, "Your kingdom come; your will be done," with the belief that it will be done by others or by a God who stands outside the world and makes history happen. Asking God to be born in us is saying, "Your kingdom, which is your presence, come into my heart. Your will be done through my life as it is done wherever you are received." Both the kingdom of God on earth and in heaven are expressions of the presence of God, and only where God is received can they be experienced.

When we ask for the holy birth within us, when we ask for the kingdom to come within our hearts, we are saying, "Don't just be above me. Don't just be with me. Reign in me! Take over. Be the Lord of my life as well as the God I worship!"

God's kingdom cannot come on earth until it first reigns in human hearts. God will not stop our wars or feed our starving neighbors without us. Without us, God will not stop the monstrous persecution, imprisonment, rape, starvation, slavery, or annihilation of Christians now going on in the world. God will not fix the moral decay fostered by those we have put in power without us taking such people out of power. And, without us, God will not teach our children values or the process of discernment between good and evil, between wisdom and folly.

God uses human mouths and human arms to say, "I love you. I need you. I claim you for my own." God's realm is supposed to include the earth. That is why we say, "Your kingdom come."

We hear God's call to stewardship given in the first chapter of the Bible. From that point on we are given dominion over the earth. God's message seems to be "I am making you responsible for what happens to the earth and in the world. I'll be here to guide, inspire, and strengthen you, but I will not force you to do my will." It is as though God says, "I will not do my work in spite of you, without you, or instead of you. You are indispensable to my plan. I want to love through you." This is the whole point of life.

It will be when we allow God into our hearts that God will stop our wars, feed our hungry, stop persecution, change our morals, and more—through our lives. Both Augustine and the author of the *Theologia Germanica* said, in essence, "Without God I can do nothing. Without us, God will do nothing."[18]

Christ must be born where we are, in our time, in order to change and use our lives for our own sake and for the sake of others.

When Christ gets to the very roots of our being, he has gotten past our words and our deeds to that place, that consciousness, from which our words and deeds proceed. Look at the Sermon on the Mount in Matthew 5–7 to see how hard Jesus worked to get this point across. It is out of the heart, out of our intentions, out of our deepest desires that our words and works proceed. Actions and even appearances reflecting the will of God come from the self-given heart.

Our lives are ours to give back to God. And we love God with the very love God gives us. Perhaps that is what Luther meant when he said we could not give God anything. All we give we have received. And the most genuine gift is the self-given heart.

We find that same message all through the Christian story. "Our wills are ours to make them thine," an old prayer says. Mary, in response to the angel announcing that fearful but wonderful happening within her being, simply answered, "Let it be with me according to your word" (Luke 1:38). That was a yes with profound implications.

Such a letting go of security for simplicity of life can be desperately difficult. Jesus agonized before his crucifixion: "Not my will, but thine be done" (Luke 22:42). Had such circumstances been suddenly thrust upon him, it would have been hard enough. But he knew beforehand what could happen, and he willingly walked toward it, "setting his face toward Jerusalem."

In each of these cases there is the consent of the human will to the will of God. The Third Council of Constantinople, in 381, declared that Christ possessed both a human and a divine will. He was able to fulfill his task on earth only because his human will was utterly offered to the will of his Father. It came only with struggle. But it ended in peace.

When Luther wrote "Faith is the yes of the heart, a confidence on which one stakes one's life," he was saying faith is a response of the whole self to God. It is not just our words: the creeds we confess, the prayers we pray, the way we argue our faith, or what we say in teaching our children. It is not just our works and deeds: our faithful attendance at church, our participation on committees, or our acts of love toward others.

This yes is an inner assent of the will. It is a willingness to receive the grace and the guidance of God. It can be so deep and far-reaching as to cause a real conversion of life, a real repentance, a turning around to go in a completely new direction. It always involves, says Luther, the daily death of the person we have been in order to fulfill our reason for being alive: to accomplish God's will in our time and place.

RECEIVING CHRIST

When Christ is born in the heart, we are reborn. We become new creatures. John 1:12 reads: "To all who received him, who believed in his name, he gave power to become children of God." Powerful words! They make very clear that faith is not just a matter of believing rational propositions about God but a dynamic relationship built on God's great love, poured out to us, received by our hearts, and expressed in our lives. Luther himself said:

> Faith alone lays hold of the promise, believes God when He gives the promise, stretches out its hand when God offers something, and accepts what He offers. This is the characteristic function of faith alone.[19]

If indeed faith is extending the hand to accept what God is offering, it is a yielding, a surrender, an offering of the will to God that God may use it. This is very different from self-driven willpower. In fact, faith is the only means to do what we were commanded to do: follow, obey, and love others as Christ loves us.

We cannot do the will and work of God, but God can do it through us. We cannot continue the incarnation, but the Child, born in us, can continue the work. God can do what God would do if God lived in our shoes, in our family, in our town, in our church, with our talents and our job, in our society. God can do what God would do in spite of our humanity and through our humanity. Were we not created to be the tools of God? Ephesians 3:14-21 answers:

> I bow my knees before the Father, . . . that . . . he may grant that you may be strengthened in your inner being with power through his Spirit, and that Christ may dwell in your hearts through faith, as you are being rooted and grounded in love. I pray that you may have the power to comprehend, with all the saints, what is the breadth and length and height and depth, and to know the love of Christ that surpasses knowledge, so that you may be filled with all the fullness of God.
>
> Now to him who by the power at work within us is able to accomplish abundantly far more than all we can ask or imagine, to him be glory in the church and in Christ Jesus to all generations, forever and ever. Amen.

A Children's Hymn

I Will Make My Heart a Cradle

1 I will make my heart a cra-dle, make my lit-tle Lord a bed.

Come, Lord Je-sus, live with-in me; in my heart now lay your head.

2 Though the night is dark around me,
   all my heart is full of light.
   You are shining there, Lord Jesus,
   with your love so warm and bright.

3 Make my heart your home, Lord Jesus.
   Help me share your shining light.
   Fill me, use me, live within me.
   Love through me with all your might.

4 Use my heart to love all people.
   Use my life to live for you.
   Use my church and use my country
   to touch, to teach, to heal for you.

© *Text and music: Grace Adolphsen Brame*
Harmonization: Gordon Turk

LOVING WITH BOTH
HEAD AND HEART

BELIEF AND TRUST

"I want to believe, but I can't," agonizes my friend. He reads and reads, seeking the God he cannot name. Yet I see God's spirit in him, reaching out in beauty and blessing friends with joy. His mental agony is private. He cannot connect his head and heart, nor does he realize that on the deepest level, he loves the God he cannot understand.

Many of my friends who are confused about the reality of God seem unclear about the relationship of experience and explanation, knowing God personally and knowing about God objectively. I understand my friends. More than once, I have "been there."

The *Shema Yisroel*, Israel's only creed, tries to connect all our complicated human aspects under one priority, saying, "Hear, O Israel: The LORD is our God, the LORD alone. You shall love the LORD your God with all your heart, and with all your soul, and with all your might" (Deuteronomy 6:4-5). But when the Gospels quote Jesus' use of it, another phrase is added: "You shall love the Lord your God . . . with all your mind" (Mark 12:30). Why make such an addition? Surely it is to get the point across to a more cosmopolitan audience, even to those who think like Greeks.[1]

From a Hebrew point of view, the *Shema* was complete. For the ancient Jews, the heart, not the head, was the location of reason, intellect, mind, and will. But the Gospels make sure that everyone gets the message. "Love God!" they urge. "Love with all you are and all you have: head, heart, body, and soul. Love with your whole being!"

Focusing particularly on Jesus' addition, we might very well say, "Don't ignore your mind. Give God neither a mindless faith nor empty, rational, ineffective belief."

TWO KINDS OF FAITH

Without a balance of two kinds of faith, anyone can lose his or her way. We need both belief and trust. We need to know *about* God and to know God personally. We need to think about God with the minds God gave us and experience and express God with our whole selves.[2] Martin Buber, the twentieth-century Jewish existentialist, said that belief is objectively "acknowledging a thing to be true" and faith is "a contact of my whole being with the one I can trust." The Hebrew word for knowing God is the same as that used for the complete physical and emotional commitment of marriage: to be touched and to intimately belong to another. Both kinds of faith are vitally important: objective, clear, critical reflection and evaluation, as well as trusting, intimate relationship with another, whether a beloved person or God.[3]

As noted in the introduction, we might call these two kinds of faith "the faith of the head" and "the faith of the heart." Or we could speak of them as the principal approaches of theology on one hand and spirituality on the other. Theology is expressed in statements, propositions, and creeds. Spirituality, although it uses theology extensively, is based on our relationship to God through prayer and letting God live and love through us.

Each type of faith is different, yet they need each other and they belong together. If we believe something, it means nothing unless we live what we believe. That is "lived theology." And if we truly trust God, it should not be without reason. We might call that "reasonable faith" or "reflective spirituality." Our minds are a gift, given to us to use as far as they will take us. But they will not take us past mystery, and they can never explain God's love. Those can only be experienced. And in God's presence, they do not need to be explained.

The objectivity of theology is deeply needed. It asks what is historically and logically true. It clarifies, evaluates, and compares. It protects from naiveté. It systematizes thought, building it into a reasonable order. It gives words to concepts so that belief can be verbally expressed and passed on. It attempts to "make sense" of everything. It is irreplaceable in true education.

But religion has to do not only with what makes sense or what really happened or what "works" to make life fulfilling. It touches on experiences and mysteries that are real, that grasp us at our deepest levels and affect our lives profoundly: the incomprehensibility of life, of love, of birth and death, and of life eternal; of meaning and our reason for being alive; of differences, estrangement, and sin; and of the strange interweaving of good and evil, of the beautiful and sordid, of light and darkness.

Yes, we need both head and heart. Most of us recognize that if either belief or trust is taken to extremes, they are not only inadequate, but they can actually harm. The extremes of belief and trust are rationalism and fideism.

Rationalism is a dependence upon reason alone. It has been used to reject revelation and even to reject all religious belief. It is easily guilty of reductionism: looking at things so simplistically that one confuses a part for the whole, mistaking an aspect of truth for the complete truth. Rationalism may confuse the container with the content: that is, it may confuse appearance with reality, essence, or meaning. In fastening on reason alone, as is appropriately attempted with the scientific method, rationalism perceives the obvious, the measurable, the definable, and perhaps repeatable, but it often does not recognize levels of meaning. Nor can it, because of its effort to be objective, experience relationship.

Rationalism says that nothing can be believed that cannot be logically proved. A rationalist cannot believe in anything beyond what the mind can handle or the senses perceive. This is true even though all of these are subject to illusion as well.

To hold the rationalist's view is to say that only what a human can conceive (based on actual fact), understand, and analyze is real. Everything else is a matter of imagination or wish. Rationalism says we have created God in our own minds. It cannot comprehend that it could have been the other way around.

But faith is extreme when it is truly blind to reason and will not deal with logic or limitations, self-centeredness or even evil, thinking that things as they are are the revealed will of God. Faith is extreme when it says reason is useless, when it contends that God cannot teach us through our minds.

This type of faith is known as fideism. It is the kind of faith that causes parents to deny medical treatment to a dying child because they believe God must heal without using the gifts and people God has given. It is exemplified in people who handle poisonous snakes to prove their faith. Fideism says, "God can do anything!" and assumes that if one truly believes, whatever happens will be the will of God. It does not ask whether God thinks it wise to do everything for us, crippling us as spoiled children are crippled, robbing us of responsibility, ability, and choice.

Fideism *demands* of God divine action from outside the natural world. It presumes that doing anything for ourselves is interfering with the will of God rather than cooperating with it. It does not recognize that God wants to work through us and has given us the inspiration, gifts, and responsibility to be channels of divine grace (as in Genesis 1:27). It does not understand that God is far closer than we realize: thinking, even reasoning, within our own minds, reaching out through the skill of a doctor or scientist, and teaching us through many different lips when we can discern well enough to hear.

It is true that Luke 10:19 says to us: "I have given you authority to tread on snakes and scorpions, . . . and nothing will hurt you." But there is nothing in that passage to suggest that believers should purposely put the lives God has given them into danger, daring God to save them. Jesus refuted that devilish idea when he refused to throw himself from the top of the temple in order to prove that God, by means of angels, would come to his aid.

Evelyn Underhill wrote in *The Life of the Spirit and the Life of Today*, "When a great truth has become exaggerated . . . and is held to the exclusion of its completing opposite, it is on a fair way to becoming a lie."[4] Held in sensible balance, trust and belief can be seen for their individual worth and can be correctives and completions of each other.

Luther, however, who was born following the most extreme period of scholasticism, did not at all consider reason and trust to be equal. Often he railed against reason and called it "a whore." In the scholasticism with which he was familiar, he perceived an arrogance in its understanding that human, objective, philosophical logic alone was sufficient. In a sermon, he once stated baldly, "Reason is directly opposite to faith. It must be killed and buried in believers. . . . Reason cannot comprehend the articles of faith." Then he challenged his congregation, "How can children believe, seeing that as yet they have no reasoning power?" And his answer was instantaneous: "This is exactly why children can believe better. . . . I must become a child, must let myself be carried, touched, and blessed by Christ."[5]

Although Luther was a supreme polemicist and deeply respected reason when used as God's tool, his heart's primary response to the presence and promise of grace was trust. The gift of reason alone could never have sustained him through his difficult sixty-three years.

All of us live with challenges to our faith. Each of us muddles through life learning to trust and believe. Two of the challenges I faced in learning to recognize and live with these two kinds of faith follow.

CHALLENGE #1:
LEARNING TO LIVE WITH HEAD AND HEART

I was a first-year student at college and, like freshmen everywhere, was still sorting out my values as I made decisions without my parents. I asked God to show me what mattered. It was a time of "spiritual discernment," but I had no words for it then. It was exciting, even exhilarating. But some real pain was waiting for me just around the corner.

Somewhere in the midst of the first semester I was brought up short by a life-changing question in my mind. It challenged me to the core. "How do you know your faith is really yours?" it asked. "Maybe it's just inherited from your parents. Maybe you just *think* you believe, because someone else has given you the answers. Maybe you trust their teaching because you trust them. But that is trusting them. It is not trusting God."

The inner questions went on. "Who or what is your ultimate authority? Your parents or professors, the church or the Bible, your logic or your experience?" And others might have added "Your friends, your sorority or fraternity, the media, or culture?"

That question was difficult to face. I wanted to hold onto the firm foundation my parents had given me and the answers that I already had. I depended on my faith and didn't want it to change. I thought that if I dared to question what I had been taught, my whole world would crumble. But I couldn't avoid the challenge. Neither could I dismiss the positive relationships that I trusted. At the time, my questions concerned what I believed, not my relationship with

God, which guided, strengthened, and inspired me. The challenge that I faced was about my cognitive understanding of that relationship. And yet they were so connected! My belief undergirded my relationship with God. What would happen if my answers changed? Would my relationship with God disappear? How could I love or depend on something that was not real or true?

I knew no one to whom I could take my questions. I am not sure I could have even asked them. They threatened the very stability of my life. There seemed to be no way to solve them except to pray for help and then to be quiet and receptive to the guidance God would give me.

After several very difficult weeks, I discovered with great joy that I had not lost what I valued most. But I was much more clear about one thing: only God is God. The wisest parents are not God. The church is not God. Even the Bible is not God. They tell us about God. They even put us in touch with God. And, we hope, we find God speaking to us through them. If we are fortunate, they reveal the true reality behind all life, but they are not the reality itself. I needed to listen, not only to them, but to the Holy Spirit when it spoke through them. I also needed to listen in prayerful silence.

Years later, as I taught my first college class in theology, I challenged my students as I had been challenged. "I will not tell you what to believe," I said. "This class is here for you to make up your own mind, because your faith must be truly your own. But I will tell you what teachers of the church have taught through the centuries. I will challenge your thinking while supporting your effort. I will give you help in your prayer life, your worship, and your discernment, if you wish it. Sometimes I will tell you what I believe, but I will never insist you agree. In the end, I want you to know far better than you do today what really has worth to you. I want you to know what the Lutheran philosophical theologian Paul Tillich would have called your "ultimate concern."[6]

Help from Fowler and Luther

Fortunately for me, I began to teach after James Fowler wrote his book *The Stages of Faith*. Little in my teaching experience has been as helpful for people of all backgrounds. In the book Fowler traces normal growth in faith from infancy to adolescence and through three potential steps beyond.[7]

It was at the conjunction of his stages three and four, toward the end of adolescence, that I had been challenged. Stage three is the time when Fowler thinks that we see all authority as outside ourselves and stage four as the time when we claim our own authority. Thomas A. Droege, summarizing Fowler's work, suggests that people at stage three declare, "I believe what the church believes."[8]

Looking at that statement, many of us would agree that there is a time for all of us when the authority of some institution or person assumes superiority for us. Parent, priest, professor, or some hero seems to have the "answers" we need for living. In fact, answers are very important. At that stage it could bring imbalance to think of true faith as open-ended.

Toward the beginning of this period, most Christians are confirmed. Fowler suggests that many people never pass beyond this point of understanding.

Had I had the opportunity to study Fowler at the time of my own challenge, I would have been supported in my discovery that to base my belief on the authority of my superiors is to believe primarily in them, not in someone or something greater than they.

Luther certainly knew this. For him the ultimate authority was the life-giving Word. That was not just the Bible.[9] He saw the Word speaking at creation and through the message and the life of Christ. He saw it moving and guiding through the Holy Spirit.

In a letter to the church at Frankfurt, Luther decries the exact words employed by Droege in describing Fowler's third stage: "I believe what the church believes."[10] In a Christmas sermon he heatedly responds: "God grant us very little of that sort of faith." He says of the Word:

> Whoever accepts it on account of a preacher, believes neither the Word, nor in God through the Word; but believes the preacher and in the preacher. . . . The Word itself, disregarding the person, must satisfy the heart, must embrace and capture the man so that he, like one who is imprisoned in it, feels how true and right it is.[11]

Paul Tillich comments even more strongly:

> The Christian may believe the biblical writers, but not unconditionally. He does not have faith in them. He should not even have faith in the Bible. For faith is more than trust in even the most sacred authority. It is participation in the subject of one's

ultimate concern with one's whole being. Therefore the term 'faith' should not be used in connection with theoretical knowledge, . . . or . . . on the basis of trust in authorities.[12]

Perhaps Luther's most forceful remarks on this subject are in response to Habakkuk 2:4: "The righteous live by their faith." To that he adds: "Let no one hope to be saved by another's faith or work. This cannot be done even through . . . Christ's work and faith, but only through your own faith."[13]

Throughout the Gospel of John, Jesus speaks of the authority on which he depends. In John 12:49 he states: "I have not spoken on my own, but the Father who sent me has himself given me a commandment about what to say and what to speak." Jesus himself trusted in the deepest and truest authority, the authority of God. He was open to it in prayer and in his prayerful life.

Trusting in the Living Word

Our own trust is fed by the living Word. On that we can depend. Luther once asserted:

> Only one thing is necessary for the Christian life, the most holy Word of God. . . . The soul can do without anything except the Word of God and . . . where the Word is missing, there is no help at all for the soul.[14]

These words from "The Freedom of a Christian" obviously do not speak simply of hearing the Word with our ears, or even with our minds, but of hearing at the deepest level, with a receptive heart. Luther strongly asserted that "an idea without a corresponding experience in the depths of the heart" is not faith.[15]

The biblical text has no power by itself. "The commandments show us what we ought to do," writes Luther, "but do not give us the power to do it." It is only God's Word ruling in the soul by faith that will give that power. "Just as the heated iron glows like fire because of the union of fire with it, so the Word imparts its qualities to the soul. . . . Then a Christian has all he [or she] needs."[16] It is the Spirit that speaks in the Word. Olivier Clement of France, a contemporary Eastern Orthodox theologian, teaches, "While listening to the Word the heart is touched by a particular saying and set on fire. Then one must stop and let the fire spread quietly."[17]

The God in whom our faith is centered is not just a mental construct but is, as both Augustine and Anselm of Canterbury said, far beyond all that we can think or even imagine. We do not create God by our theology. On the contrary, it is because we actually encounter God that we try to understand what has happened and attempt to explain it theologically.

Let us say it even more simply. If we talk about a God who does not exist, God is only an idea. It is, however, the other way around. God's existence calls forth our explanation. God must, in some way, relate to us, reach out to us, touch us, and reveal God's self before we can respond or analyze what has happened.

That encounter is what Luther refers to when, following John 6:45, he states that our greatest need is not to be taught information about God, but to be "taught by God" in our hearts, to experience God intuitively. In "The Freedom of a Christian," Luther writes, "God teaches us inwardly through the living instruction of his Spirit. . . . There is need of the prayer that the Lord . . . may make us *theodidacti*, that is, those taught by God, and . . . write his law in our hearts; otherwise there is no hope for us."[18] Strong words!

A thousand years before Luther, Augustine poignantly wrote of that same inner hearing of God's word:

> Here there is a great mystery. Your ears are touched by the sound of my words, but the master is within. We may instruct you by the sound of our voice, but, if there is no one teaching you within, then the sound that we make is in vain. . . . You have one master, the Christ.[19]

And Luther says more:

> No one can understand God or his Word if he has not been enlightened by the Holy Spirit. The action of the Holy Spirit has to be experienced, sustained, and felt, and it is in undergoing these experiences that one passes through the school of the Holy Spirit. If one has not gone through it, words remain no more than words. We can know God only through the work that he does in us.[20]

Prayerful Reading

The first Christian theology was dependent upon this point of view, for theology was derived from study of Hebrew Scripture and those Christian texts that were held in highest esteem. They were to be read prayerfully, receptively, as though God was truly speaking through the pages. Thus the procedure was known in monastic circles as "divine reading," *lectio divina*. Study was prayer, a living communication from God, thoughtfully and trustingly received by the reader. The inspired texts, like Christ, were seen as a living Word, offered "to us" and "for us."

To read and study the Bible in this way is very different from today's normal academic study, where we analyze and compare what various scholars throughout history have said about the original message. Its immediacy, where appropriate, is very different from scrutinizing a passage for the date it was written or making assumptions about the author, the author's goal in writing, or the intended audience. It may not take into account the culture whose words and ways and understandings were part of its expression. It may not compare differences between various passages of scripture. It definitely does not enter into theological arguments. In short, *lectio divina* is not doing systematic theology. Nor is it analytical Bible study.

And yet such prayerful reading can be followed or even combined with a more academic approach. Our present-day critical-historic method is extremely valuable. It cannot be ignored without great cost. Combined with prayerful reading, an integrated life of faith is possible.

Lectio divina is an important bridge between academia and the personal life of faith, between theology and spirituality. It is a means to love God with both the mind and heart. It is a discipline that depends upon the leading of the Holy Spirit.

Luther once explained that we know the Bible is true because we experience the Spirit speaking through its pages.[21] He contended, "God must say to you in your heart that this Word is God's Word, otherwise it is uncertain."[22]

We are told in John 14:25 that the Holy Spirit "will teach [us] all things." Karl Barth once explained those words by saying that the Spirit "is God in us, allowing and enabling us to believe and to receive the Word as the Word of God, to share in God's revelation of himself and to speak of Christ as the Word made flesh."[23] This must mean that when the Holy Spirit is our teacher, both our devotional life and our academic study will be transformed.

CHALLENGE #2:
SYMBOLS POINT TO TRUTH

By the time I went to seminary, I thought I could handle the academic religious world. But I was unprepared for what happened one day in a class on Rudolf Bultmann's "demythologization of the New Testament." I had believed all my life that most things in the Bible were literally true. To be told that much of it might well be an expression of believers' faith, in contrast to actual fact, was a very different way of understanding Scripture. But when Bultmann stripped away the literal understanding of the miraculous, all in one hour's time, it was shattering to me. I was lost.

When the lecture was over, I ran to my room. Getting down on my knees by my cot I cried out words I had heard repeatedly but never understood. Still not understanding, I nevertheless knew they said what I felt: "Lord, I believe. Help my unbelief!" (Mark 9:24 KJV)

It was agony, even a kind of death. And it lasted at least half a year. But what it taught me was that I was not dependent on the literal inerrancy of the Bible. My faith was in the living God, whom I knew and experienced. This was the God who had inspired those who wrote the Bible. This was the God who spoke to me through its pages. And this was the God who touched me and guided me in the silence of prayer, in the glory of music, in the tenderness of human love, and in the awesomeness of nature. This was the God who entered human history and entered human hearts. This was the God who claimed me in love forever.

I discovered that God was not bound by a cage of words. God was not to be imprisoned by descriptions or narratives. All of these were there to point to the inexpressible, awesome, but immanent, God, but they could never limit, define, or put conceptual boundaries around this one on whom our faith is built. Words are symbols of what they describe and represent, just as are music and art. As Tillich taught, they point to the holy, and we even participate in the holy by means of them.[24] But they cannot enclose it, for the holy is always greater than the symbol that conveys it. Otherwise the symbol itself becomes an idol, and I worship it and not that of which it speaks.

The words of Scripture; the water, bread, and wine of baptism and communion; a cross or stained-glass window; a mountain or a flower; a sunset or a starry night: all these say, "There is more! You are in touch with it now."

Years later I realized that my confusion had once again been between what I believed and my personal experience of God. When I had said, "Lord, I believe," I really meant, "Lord, I trust you. I believe in you. I love you!" And when I had said, "Help my unbelief," I meant, "Clear up my mental confusion! I do not understand!"

I did not realize then that I had entered Fowler's fourth stage, which ushers in a time of individuation, perhaps of rebelliousness, respect for one's own way of thinking, and a new ability to reflectively evaluate. It may also bring a "demythologization" when "meanings are separated from the symbols that bear them." That means that symbolic truth can be distinguished from literal fact. Meaning can be distinguished from the historical reality of an event or story.

Yes, I had entered Fowler's fourth stage, but not by my own volition. I was pushed! If, in all these circumstances, I had understood the difference between reasoned belief and trust, it would have helped greatly. It took even longer for me to understand how they were related to the fields of theology and spirituality. For years, although it was the foundation of my life, I did not know what spirituality was. It had no name. I have not been alone.

Theology and Spirituality

Let us begin with the term easier to define. What is theology? The study of God? Disciplined thinking about God? "The ordered effort to bring our experience of God to intelligent expression" as Richard McBrien explains?[25] Is it "faith seeking understanding," as Anselm would say? Is it an explanation, as far as objective reason and analytical logic can take us, of the source of life and the mysteries of meaning and purpose? Is it a critical inquiry into what is beyond and more than the life that we can empirically know?

If it is any or all of these, it cannot stand alone. If God is only an idea, a concept, something or someone we talk about but never experience, then we create God, and there are as many gods as there are theologies. If God is something or someone only exterior, outside ourselves, to be objectively analyzed by effects in nature and history or if God is only an innate, mechanical, self-unfolding process, that God can claim no personal response, no love or dedication.

If God is that to whom we consciously belong and to whom we are personally committed, however, then God is God in our hearts and not just a concept we examine with our minds. Then the experience of God is primary and motivates theology, which, thus understood, is a rational attempt to understand that transformative experience and its expression.

Although there is a basic consensus on the meaning of the word *theology* across the Christian world, the same cannot be said of the term *spirituality*. Until the 1980s, most people, especially Protestants, did not even know what it was, and even now, few could define it appropriately. We simply lack education. Even academics often misunderstand it. They have never had a course in its history, the spiritual classics, contemplative or meditative prayer, the spiritual journey, or the integration of theology and spirituality. The media alone informs many people about the field. the general public's inappropriate use of the word, however, does not keep true spirituality from existing. An intelligent person simply needs to look past the public press.

Every religious group has its own spirituality, whether it uses the term or not. And each person in the group has his or her own spirituality as well. It may be sick or healthy, naive or informed, world-denying or -affirming, self-centered or loving. It surely is all of these at one time or another.

The word *spirituality*, as it is used in this writing, points to healthy, balanced, incarnate, world-affirming, self-giving, and receptive living under the guidance of the Spirit. It refers to the individual; to the body of Christ, the church; and to society. None of them should be slighted, as we have done too often in the past.

Faith as the experience of trust is what spirituality is all about. Spirituality refers, first of all, to the work of the Holy Spirit in human hearts and lives, beginning with the Spirit's call. Thus it includes the human response to the Spirit: gratitude for grace, the "turning around" of repentance and conversion, discipline and sacrifice and commitment, ways of life and worship, and the empowerment of others by liberating, supporting, and sustaining them.

We might say that the primary definition of *spirituality* is the experience and the expression of the Holy Spirit in, among, and through individuals and groups. It is visible through a way of life and worship, through concern for the earth and justice for all people expressed through loving service, and is inspired and guided by the Spirit.

In the pre-Reformation church, spirituality was taught only to the "religious": priests, monks, and nuns. The whole idea of spirituality for everyone, although attempted a number of times in history, is primarily a late twentieth-century phenomenon. Before that, although their effort was to live life guided by the Holy Spirit, some lay spirituality movements were distrusted and their members sometimes called "heretics," derided, imprisoned, or even killed. The Christian church needs to look once again at these movements, and, instead of focusing on what was lacking among some, to see what their lasting gifts have been to us.[26]

SUMMARY

The aim of this chapter has been to see how believing and trusting can be integrated. Eastern Orthodoxy can help us find our way. To the Orthodox, a true theologian is not simply a person who applies reason and logic to the understanding and explanation of God or to the Word of God. The real theologian is one in whom the Word of God, the *theou logos*, lives, using that individual life as its instrument.[27]

All that we say "about God" is only conjecture if the experience of God is not its foundation. We speak of that which we love, which we are ever growing to "know personally," not scientifically, but experientially. Otherwise our knowledge is hollow and our words are "like a noisy gong or a clanging cymbal" (1 Corinthians 13:1). We simply "cannot, by [our] own reason or effort" teach, preach, or do the works of mercy without it.

We are not saved by our theology. Nor are we saved by our spirituality. We are saved (healed, made whole, and freed from bitterness, fear, and arrogance) by the grace of the Holy Spirit. It breathes itself into every cranny of our being and every corner of our lives in order to be received in trust.

THE HEART CALLED
AND OFFERED

GIVING WHAT WE RECEIVE

In *Preface to Romans*, Martin Luther wrote, "All Christians are priests. . . . The sacrifices they offer are their own selves."[1] We are called, called to love God with every bit of our being, called to love others as much as ourselves. We are called from loneliness to relationship. And in that relationship we become alive.

Nothing is more important than hearing the call of God. If we miss it, we do not understand why we are here on earth. And yet the call comes every moment that we breathe.

"Thou shalt love" is behind everything that gives life and holds the world together. God's very self, poured out in love and given before we could ask, is ours. We are called to pass it on. The call comes from the very one who provides our ability to hear and answer it. Wondrously, that call is never without God's gifts, and the one who gives both call and gifts never takes them back. "The gifts and the calling of God are irrevocable" (Romans 11:29). We give back only that which was first given, and our truest offerings are our selves.

It is sometimes difficult to understand how the same Luther could write "All Christians are priests. . . . The sacrifices they offer are their own selves" (which is an act of love) and then sound as though he were saying we cannot love God. But Luther often divides nature from grace so completely that we do not get his whole message. In his second book on Galatians, Luther writes:

> [Our] spiritual endowments are . . . corrupt, . . . totally extin-
> guished through sin. . . . Whatever is in our will is evil; whatever

67

is in our intellect is error. In divine matters, therefore, man has nothing but darkness, error, malice, and perversity of will and of intellect. Then how could he do good works, love God, etc.?[2]

If Luther had said only this, his argument would contradict itself. If all human intellect is in error, this statement cannot be taken seriously, for it cannot be true. We cannot think about Luther's statement, for we are sure to be wrong. Further, none of us should dare to do theology, since our intellect is perverse as well.

Were we to follow only this statement of Luther's, life would seem utterly hopeless. We would believe we could not love God or neighbor. Then why live?

It is extremely important to note that Luther's complete view is not that we cannot love God or others, do good works, or use reason. He emphasized that all of us are naturally self-centered. Egocentricity separates us from God, but grace makes the difference.[3] Whatever good we do is done by the Holy Spirit in us, by grace received (Philippians 4:13). This grace, God's love to us and through us, comes abundantly! Luther writes of God's nature as "nothing but the intense fire and fervor of a love that has *filled* heaven and earth"[4] (emphasis added).

There is no such thing as nature without grace, or life on earth would be extinct. Job 34:14-15 says succinctly:

> If he should take back his spirit to himself,
> and gather to himself his breath,
> all flesh would perish together,
> and all mortals return to dust.

We cannot be born without grace, and we cannot exist without it. We are created, sustained, and completed by grace. That is why we speak of faith in the same breath with grace. Faith is the breathing in of God's breath. It is faith that receives grace, that trusts and depends on grace, and that opens the heart to all that God continuously and faithfully gives.

GIFTED AND CALLED FOR OTHERS

To be called is to be asked to fill a need, a need that we care about, perhaps to the point of passion, a need that we, in particular, are potentially fitted to address, but before which we may well feel inadequate when it is first presented.[5]

The one who loved us to life and asks entrance to the very center of our being offers us meaning for our living. The one who calls is the one who claims us. Life matters . . . everyone's! And we, ourselves, pass on the claiming and the calling, the loving and the healing, the challenging and the setting free. Our offering becomes our fulfillment!

Often, when I am giving a retreat, a mature person will confide in me that they are still looking for their calling. Even though they may have lived two-thirds of their lifetime, they still do not know why they are on earth.

I wonder sometimes if we have made the idea of call too glorious, too heroic, too dramatic, or too different from everyday life. We confess in the Nicene Creed that the Holy Spirit "has spoken through the prophets," but surely that does not mean that only prophets are called or that only "special people" can share the Word of life. What would that say to Sunday school teachers or to church members ministering to shut-ins? Furthermore, we think of the Hebrew prophets as men only. Surely that does not mean that God cannot or will not speak through women. By what criteria do we know whether someone else is called?

Except for occupations that are obviously evil and destructive, I cannot see any that are devoid of mission, devoid of the opportunity to affirm, inspire, or enrich others or to receive assistance from them.

My heart aches every time a person uses the words *only* or *just* before describing who they are or what they do. Anything good can be noble. Anything necessary is important.

Very few calls are glamorous, and once followed, a true mission is more a matter of finding God in the ordinaries of life than doing great things that the world will see or history will remember. It is a matter of using eyes to see the earth and its people as holy, that is, belonging to God. The ordinary is sacred, but the sacred is not ordinary.

A mission is a privilege, an excitement, a joy, a responsibility. When there is glory in it, the glory is God's. "Let your light shine before others, so that [when] they . . . see your good works," they will glorify God (Matt. 5:16). We are born to be transparent windows to the holy.

For some people, a call can be dramatic or visionary, an exceptional experience that will always be remembered; this does not necessarily make it more authentic. For others, it is a quietly growing but unmistakable sensitivity, concern, or compassion for some group of people or some part of the earth that needs to be loved to life. Or it may simply begin with a nudge: "Maybe it would help a bit if you lent a hand . . ." until one really sees how she or he can make a difference to someone.

A call may not always be to a specific task. Some of us are called to a particular way of doing our normal work. Our daily duties are to become transformed and transforming for others.

The word *vocation* literally means "a calling." But for too long the world has understood that only a few have vocations. Too many have been misled to believe that a true call is only to the professional ministry, to teaching or the monastery, or to some sort of vowed estate that requires a divestment of attachments but promises spiritual gain or respect. None of us should go into any ministry for the primary purpose of being a leader or "becoming holy." If we do, we will use our ministry primarily to fill our own emotional needs, to build our own self-image, even a spiritual one. Self-actualization is not a requirement for ministry, but it can be a result for those who lose themselves in love.

All were born to care for and serve each other as Christ would serve in our shoes. Commitment to do that in any situation is the real challenge. We are called to "go into all the world," not just into its pulpits and missions. The battlefields of business and finance, of politics and the media desperately need those who recognize God's call. But it takes real imagination and courage to build effective ministries there.

Christ, who came to live in the thick of things and never set himself apart, may well call us to the most secular of settings. He may ask that we say yes to following him where it is hardest of all to go but where it can really make a difference. That is why Christ's followers have been called "the salt of the earth." Christlike love is needed everywhere to flavor and to enhance life, to preserve it and keep it from rotting, even to cleanse and heal.

But just because we have been called does not mean that we will find it easy or safe. The church was built on the blood of the martyrs, people who loved God passionately and gave their lives that the kingdom would come on earth. It still is.

Many calls really are heroic, but most people on the outside will never guess their cost, and from the inside, heeding those calls is a matter of being doggedly faithful, regardless of our weaknesses, inadequacies, and fear.

All of the great prophets of scripture began as ordinary people who were asked to reveal the extraordinary in the midst of tremendous challenge. All of them felt inadequate. All of them gave excuses. All of them seemed to be afraid.

INADEQUATE PROPHETS

Nothing is so intriguing among Bible stories as accounts of the call of God and the frightened response of most of those to whom it was addressed. For them there was a terrible feeling of inadequacy in the face of an awesome challenge.

There is Moses, alone on a mountain with his father-in-law's sheep and a flaming bush that speaks for God! This is a frightened Moses, who even takes off his shoes when he is told he is on holy ground. This is a man who is afraid to look up for fear he will see the face of the Almighty. And God speaks to him: "Go, Moses! Go down to Pharaoh and demand the release of your people!"

Moses had no trouble questioning God's choice as fast as he could get the words out! "Who do you think I am, God, to send me to the Pharaoh?" In the book of Exodus, the conversation goes on for another chapter and a half with Moses still protesting to the end: "Oh Lord, I'm not good at talking, and you know I don't do well in front of people! Please send someone else!" (Exodus 3–4).

Then there is the wonderful story of Isaiah in the temple. Surrounded by smoke, which veiled the awesome glory of God, engulfed in a sense of holiness beyond all imagining, he must have fallen to his knees. Music filled the temple: the voices of angels singing, "Holy, holy, holy," the first Sanctus. Then through the screen of smoke he saw the Lord, "high and lofty," with angels on every side.

Overcome, Isaiah cried, "I'm not good enough to see all this! I'm sinful! My speech is my sin! You know how I talk! You know what I say! I do not have a prophet's mouth. My lips are unclean, and all my friends and family have unclean lips as well!" (Isaiah 6).

There is also the story of Jeremiah, probably just a teenager when his story begins. He is described by some writers as "warm-hearted, affectionate, not given to strife, timid in spirit, with the sensibilities of a poet."[6] But the Lord spoke to him, saying, "Before I formed you in the womb I knew you, and before you were born I consecrated you." God was saying: "I chose you for my purpose."

What was Jeremiah's response? "Oh God, I don't know how to talk! I'm not even grown up yet! I'm only a kid!" (Jeremiah 1).

To each of these three people, Yahweh, the Lord, gave a similar response. To Moses he said, "Go! And I will be with your mouth and teach you what to speak!" To Isaiah he answered, "I will cleanse your lips with fire! I will forgive your sin. And I will take away your guilt!" To Jeremiah he replied, "Don't tell me you're just a kid! To whomsoever I send you, you will go, and whatsoever I command you, you will speak. Don't be afraid, for I am with you, and I have put my words in your mouth!"

In story after story of the call from God, the weak and timid response has been "Oh God! Who . . . me?"

WHO IS CALLED?

There may be many of us who are quite relieved that we have not been called to be prophets! But that does not mean we have not been called.

Scripture makes it quite clear that we have all been called. We are "called to be saints": that means people whose lives are given to God. The words Christ spoke to the disciples are spoken to us: "You did not choose me but I chose you. And I appointed you to go and bear fruit, fruit that will last!" (John 15:16). Our ordination, says Luther, is in our baptism. And the ordination is to "the priesthood of all believers," "the universal priesthood."[7]

We are part of the body of Christ, and wherever we are, all of us together are called to do what Christ would have done, had he remained here in the flesh. Jesus even said that he expects us to do more than he would have! "The one who believes in me . . . will do greater works than these, because I am going to the Father" (John 14:12). How could that be possible?

Jesus answers before we can ask. He says, "I will send you the Spirit, the Comforter," literally the one who comes "with strength." That Spirit will guide us, not from the outside, as Christ had done as friend and master, but from inside, something the unbelieving world could never comprehend. "The Spirit will not only be with you," he says, "but will be in you." He goes on to tenderly say that if we love him and keep his word, the Father and he will come to us and make their "home" within us (John 14:17, 23). Yes, we are called. And we are empowered to open our hearts that his Spirit may come in, making its home in us.

Luther refers to the call of all people in his *Small Catechism*, a book written for fathers to use in teaching their families. In his explanation to the Third Article of the Apostles' Creed are some of Luther's most memorable words:

> I cannot, by my own understanding or effort, believe in Jesus Christ my Lord, or come to Him. But *the Holy Spirit has called me* through the Gospel, enlightened me with his gifts, and sanctified and kept me in true faith. In the same way he *calls*, gathers, enlightens, and sanctifies *the whole Christian Church* on earth.[8] (emphasis added)

There is no one whose life does not belong to God and is not claimed for God's use. There is no life that has no purpose and no meaning. There is no one without a gift to give.

The power to say yes to God is given with God's call, and to obey that call is to truly hear. Obeying is doing what God would do if God were in our skin. It is willing the will of God, wanting the will of God. Our strength is inspired by the will of God.

Obeying is also risking—maybe everything. What we believe and live for, others may misunderstand, scorn, ignore, or even destroy. Our name may be blackened, our work blackballed or minimized, our job not renewed. But if we don't risk sharing our gift, will our lives have meaning? Will we have done what we came to do? What would be worse than missing it all?

WHO DO WE THINK WE ARE?

We become what we are to be by taking risks, by daring, by falling on our faces like an infant learning to walk. And we become what we are to be by learning what love is and how to do it wisely, helpfully, one lesson after another.

There are many who would stop us. Through the mouths of adversaries and even friends and family we have heard, "Who do you think you are?" When said to hurt and demean, those words do not come from God. When said to curb our passion, to put us "in our place," to rob us of confidence, they deny the power of God within us.

I can believe that who I am is based on my reputation or my family tree, my address or my bank account. I can think that who I am is how much I know, the title before my name, the degrees I have earned, the authority I bear, or the uniform I wear. I can accept the unspoken assumption of the one who taunts me: I can admit I am not much of anything. Or I can recognize that I am a child and channel of God.

Paul puts it this way in 2 Corinthians 4:7: "We have this treasure in clay jars, so that it may be made clear that this extraordinary power belongs to God and does not come from us." One day, writing in my spiritual notebook, this simple understanding was given to me:

> We were born to be nothing
> but vessels of God.
> That is all.
> And that is all!
> It is everything.

No one is born with healthy self-esteem. "Who do you think you are?" is the self-taunt that Moses, Isaiah, and Jeremiah heard inside themselves when God's call came. It was important for them to recognize where that taunt was coming from. It could have been simply the voice of caution, of wisdom. It also could have been the voice of the enemy of God. That enemy does not want us to succeed in anything life-giving. That enemy will do anything to deny the power of God within us.

I sometimes meet that negative taunt as I sit in my car outside a hospital where some friend lies in crisis. The voice inside me says, "Do you realize how bad this situation is? What difference can you make? Who do you think you are?"

God answers back to say, "That is not the issue. Do what you know to do, and let me give you each thought and each word as you need it. Just be a voice, a presence, a hand, a pair of eyes that communicates for me 'I love you, and I will never ever leave you. I will be with you always.' Then help them learn to pray in trust."

So I go in, armed with what God has taught me about receptive prayer. It is so simple, but in some way, God always uses it for good. Sometimes God amazes me.[9]

I always seem to be learning: we can have faith in God or faith in fear. When we have faith in fear, the magnificent energy that God gives us evaporates. It leaks out of us in agonizing slowness. It floods out of us in a rush. Fear robs, trespasses, usurps God's right to our lives.

What conquers fear? Putting something stronger in its place. "There is no fear in love, but perfect love casts out fear," says 1 John 4:18. "Love is letting go of fear," wrote the psychologist Gerald Jampolsky after facing a raving inmate locked alone with him in a padded cell.[10] But the raving inmate is not always outside. We can lock ourselves alone in our minds with our own inmate: fear. Fear focuses on what is wrong; love focuses on what is right. Fear focuses on weakness; love focuses on strength. Fear focuses on the self; love focuses on someone else. Fear steals our trust; love depends on trust. Fear robs us of personal integrity and self-respect; love gives life and hope away.

Going on in faith is a matter of choice, discipline, and practice, but none of these are possible without the gift of grace, nor do they compare. We are reminded that "the gifts and calling of God are irrevocable" (Romans 11:29). The gifts are promised with the call.

Two sentences speak, sing, and whisper pervasively in my being. Christ's words say, "Apart from me you can do nothing" (John 15:5). And Paul affirms, "I can do all things through him who strengthens me" (Philippians 4:13). How easy it is to forget that all power is God's! It is true: we were born to be nothing but vessels of God. That is all. And that is all. It is everything! It is our need and our glory.

GOD FILLS THE EMPTY CUP

Fear is a consciousness of our inadequacy that only God can fill. We cannot live without the love of God. We are contingent. Our very inadequacy is our blessing. Our limitations are the opportunity that causes us to yearn for the presence of God, to drink deeply of God's love, to taste God's meat and be satisfied.

The one who created us eternally gives God's own life that ours may be complete. And when we feel lost and forgotten, far away and famished, God and our hunger reach toward each other. Our hunger and need are clasped to God's waiting breast, and we are warmed and fed and healed.

The apostle Paul felt that clasp, that grasp of God. "Christ Jesus has made me his own," he triumphed (Philippians 3:12). Paul Tillich felt and understood it as the call to faith. Faith, he says, occurs when we feel ourselves "grasped" by what ultimately concerns us, what matters most. Genuine faith demands "total surrender to the subject of ultimate concern." He puts it more personally and eloquently later, saying, "Love is the power in the ground of everything that is, driving it beyond itself toward reunion with the other one and ultimately with the ground itself from which it is separated."[11]

God, of course, is the ground, the source of life, the place where we are rooted, the ultimate security on which we rest, and the source from which we drink the water of life.

There are people in desperate circumstances who, grasped by the love of God, offer God everything: life, possessions, loved ones, and their own hope and pain. Their trust is our inspiration. One such person, George Matheson, an Anglican priest, blind by eighteen, wrote a hymn on the day of his sister's wedding, when his own hopes for marriage had been dashed. These are his moving words:

> O Love that will not let me go,
> I rest my weary soul in thee;
> I give thee back the life I owe,
> That in thine ocean depths, its flow
> May richer, fuller be!
>
> O Joy that seekest me through pain,
> I cannot close my heart to thee.
> I trace the rainbow through the rain,
> And feel the promise is not vain
> That morn shall tearless be.[12]

God's fullness for our emptiness! "I give thee back the life I owe," even if it now seems empty. And when we have something in our cup, what we give is what we have received. We can receive only when we have let go, when we have offered the cup of our lives, no matter how empty or how partially full it may be.

CONSECRATION AND DEDICATION

In consecration and dedication we offer back to God the life that God first gave. The wonderful prayer of Ignatius of Loyola expresses this giving so well:

> Receive, O Lord, all my freedom, my memory, my understanding, and my will. All that I have or cherish, you have given. I return it all to you that it may be guided by your will. Only your love and grace I ask. With these I am rich and ask for nothing more.[13]

It is such utter self-giving that inspired what is perhaps the simplest and finest consecration hymn ever written. It was written by the poet and Englishwoman Frances Ridley Havergal:

> Take my life and let it be
> consecrated, Lord to thee.
> . . . .
> Take my will and make it thine.
> It shall be no longer mine
> Take my heart; it is thine own.
> It shall be thy royal throne.[14]

In our Sunday worship, we walk forward at the time of the offering, presenting gifts of money, bread, wine, and, perhaps water. They are not really ours to give. Yet it is all we have. The one who is both the Gift and the Giver receives what we bring to the family table. At that point, in a Lutheran service today, the congregation frequently prays:

> Merciful Father, we offer with joy and thanksgiving what you have first given us—ourselves, our time, and our possessions, signs of your gracious love. Receive them for the sake of him who offered himself for us, Jesus Christ, our Lord.[15]

SACRIFICE AND OBLATION

"Sacrifice," wrote Evelyn Underhill, "is a positive act. Its essence is something given; not something given up."[16] In ancient history, a sacrifice most often was a living being, ceremonially killed by a knife, its blood sacramentally used in the ritual, and its body consumed by fire. The ancient definition of a priest was based on the idea of one who was "set apart" to perform this sacrificial function and to lead in the ritual surrounding the offering.

There is no doubt why such a ceremony was performed. Latin scholars have called it *do ut des*. It literally means "I give so that you will give."[17] The community or individual who sacrificed intentionally gave up and destroyed something of value, perhaps of great value, in order to get something back, to influence the god who was worshiped. Such a "gift" is really not a gift at all, but a payment, a means of manipulating God, a "work" done in order to get something in return, a bargain made with the creator. It is divine "back-scratching."

It comes from thinking of God as one who has needs such as we have: physical, psychological, and emotional. Ancient people considered their many gods to be similar to themselves, neither perfect nor almighty. Gods were thought to be fickle, to have unpredictable whims. They couldn't really be trusted and needed to be cajoled.[18]

A later way of looking at sacrifice continues the approach of giving up something of great value, even one's own life, but not as payment or even manipulation. Rather the giving up is in order to express total devotion, complete dedication, love.

But there is another step beyond that. This is what Underhill describes as "something given, not given up." We offer our goods, our loves, and ourselves to be used by God for God's own purpose, to become instruments, tools, or channels for God. We realize that nothing is "our own," that all we possess, care for, and "are" belongs to our creator. It is simply an offering back of all that belongs to God already. Our response is the simplest, most natural, and most joyous of all types of sacrifice. When it first occurs, it is the most exciting thing that has ever happened to us. We cannot imagine anything that could matter more or any other reason to be alive. We simply have heard God's call. So we offer. It is "an offering of the heart."

The difference between the kinds of sacrifice is clear in reading the Hebrew prophets. Hosea wrote especially sharply: "I desire steadfast love and not sacrifice, the knowledge of God rather than burnt offerings" (6:6). In other words, "Learn to love each other! Learn to know me! That will touch my heart."[19]

Instead of manipulating, pleasing, or cajoling a god who has human needs, the sacrifice of self-giving invites God to live in and through us in love. It "allows God alone to carry out his works in one's person," as Luther writes.[20] It is, say the psalms, our "freewill offering."

In Romans 12:1, sacrificial offering is the giving of our whole being to God:

> I appeal to you therefore, brothers and sisters, by the mercies of God, to present your bodies as a living sacrifice, holy and acceptable to God, which is your spiritual worship.

In responding to that passage, Luther wrote:

> The true sacrifice to God is not something outside us or belonging to us, nor something temporal or for the moment,

but it is we ourselves, forever. . . . As Prov. 23:26 says: "My son, give Me your heart."[21]

Augustine said, "It is you who lie upon the altar. It is you, your very life within the cup."[22] He was not slighting the presence of Christ in the elements of the Eucharist. He was affirming that our hearts, our lives, our selves are offered with our gifts to the one who calls us to himself and to the world. In that sense, we place ourselves and everything we are and have upon the altar of blessing where we meet him "who offered himself for us."

We love because we were loved first. We offer because we have been called. "All Christians are priests. . . . The sacrifices they offer are their own selves." A simple chant from Iona expresses it well:

> Take, O take me as I am.
> Summon out all I will be.
> Set thy seal upon my heart,
> And live in me.[23]

CHOICES OF THE HEART

How Do We Live What We Believe?

What matters? What really matters? And what matters most? Is there, in your life, an ultimate concern alongside temporal loves and commitments, people and things? What is the last thing you would want to lose? How is everything else related to that?

The question of what matters most is the question everyone asks and answers, whether consciously or not. We base our lives upon our answer. "What matters?" is the basic question of religion. To it, we each respond differently.

William Wordsworth lamented, "The world is too much with us; late and soon, getting and spending, we lay waste our powers."[1] Evelyn Underhill, in *The Spiritual Life*, commented: "We mostly spend [our] lives conjugating three verbs: to Want, to Have, and to Do. Craving, clutching, and fussing . . . we are kept in perpetual unrest."[2] None of us is exempt from the lure of accumulation, achievement, and self-actualization.

Who or what we live for affects all our other choices. The value of everything else is determined by our first priority, our goal. Knowingly or unknowingly, we are giving our lives for it now.

The apostle Paul thought he knew what it meant to search for and find what mattered most. He was "a Pharisee of the Pharisees" before he met Jesus. Learning, position, and power were his. And he was righteous; he lived by the letter of the law. But being thrown to the ground and blinded by the light of Christ was the tragedy and victory that turned his life around. Later, imprisoned and facing death for his loyalty to Christ, he wrote of his decision:

81

> Whatever gains I had, these I have come to regard as loss because of Christ. More than that, I regard everything as loss because of the surpassing value of knowing Christ Jesus my Lord. For his sake I have suffered the loss of all things, and I regard them as rubbish, in order that I may gain Christ and be found in him. . . . I want to know Christ and the power of his resurrection and the sharing of his sufferings. . . . Forgetting what lies behind and straining forward to what lies ahead, I press on toward the goal for the prize of the heavenly call of God in Christ Jesus. (Philippians 3:7-14)

The words of Paul are strong, passionate, hopeful, joyous.

The following words of Jesus are of a different tone. They challenge us to a radical letting go, a radical consecration to the one thing that matters most, our first and deepest love. They are spoken to those who have not yet come to Paul's conviction. In Mark 8:34-37 Jesus says:

> If any want to become my followers, let them deny themselves and take up their cross and follow me. For those who want to save their life will lose it, and those who lose their life for my sake, and for the sake of the gospel, will save it. For what will it profit them to gain the whole world and forfeit their life? Indeed, what can they give in return for their life?

Over and over scripture reminds us of this singleness of heart, which is a dedicated will, and this singleness of sight, which is focus. The Authorized King James Version of the Bible presents Matthew 6:22 as "If therefore thine eye be single, thy whole body shall be full of light." To say it another way: "If you focus on the one important thing, your whole life and being will be full of God's radiance."

Kierkegaard found the subject so important that he dedicated a book to it—*Purity of Heart*. Douglas Steere found it so important that he learned Danish to translate it! Kierkegaard's message was "Purity of heart is to will one thing." That one thing was the good, the will of God.[3]

But how are we to know the good? How are we to recognize what matters most? And then how are we to live what we believe? We have conflicting loyalties. We are torn between the past and the present, one relationship and another, one loyalty and another, even between conflicting "goods." We may discover in ourselves the donkey about which Plato wrote, in danger of starving to death because he could not choose between two bales of hay! Until a choice is made, there is little peace and little progress, and we have nothing left to give to others. The agony of indecision can even destroy us. Only making a choice enables us to go on creatively with far greater peace and joy.

But often we are not given a choice. Much loss is forced upon us. Then our only choice is how to respond to loss. Perhaps we respond by allowing ourselves to cry out, to grieve and to share our pain, perhaps by eventually getting involved in our own healing process, perhaps by turning in a new direction. We probably need them all, and in that order.

LETTING GO AND GOING ON

Throughout life we find ourselves not only getting and spending, but gaining and losing, receiving and giving, letting go and adding on, or letting go and going on. We experience relinquishment and then involvement, the death of one dream and the incarnation of another, the death of one relationship and the birth of others. Even emptiness leaves room for the coming of the Holy Spirit.

We cannot live fully without letting go and going on. We leave the womb in order to be born. We leave home to go to school. Parents withhold their protection to let us grow. We let go of our first family for our spouse. We let go of freedom for the sake of accomplishment. We let go of privacy for the sake of love. We let go of earthly life for the sake of heaven.

We let go of recrimination and self-pity through forgiveness. Otherwise we are trapped in the past, and life can never be new again. Jesus said, "Turn the other cheek." Why? Because until someone stops the acceleration of violence and destruction, until someone is the first to forgive, it will be impossible to have a better world. The new cannot possibly come without relinquishing the old.

One definition of hell is to be caught eternally in remembering and rehearsing old pain, to be imprisoned by the past. Those of us who keep ourselves victims of our memory are never happy or free. A new and happier life cannot be born.

All of life is letting go, even of self-image, and certainly of self-centeredness. Anything can be an idol, that is, whatever stands between God and us. We can even be our own idol, and we frequently are. We think our own will must be done. It is enormously difficult to be supple to circumstance or open to a wiser will.

The true challenge is to let our self-idolatry, our self-centeredness, die. But how is it possible to let go of our consuming passion for what we want for ourselves above all else? The only answer seems to be by becoming more interested in someone or something else. Singleness of sight and dedicated passion find a new direction.

SURRENDER AND DETACHMENT

The word often used for letting go in spirituality is *surrender*. But who wants to surrender? For most of us that means giving up, losing our dream. That is not nearly the same as letting go. For letting go involves remembering our past dreams while finding a new one and focusing on it. It is unpossessive detachment toward what one loves. So too, surrender to God does not mean yielding to a tyrant who will enslave us, but offering our lives to the one who made us, created us for a purpose and a goal. In this sense, surrender is offering life back to the one who had the original dream for our lives. It is not losing, but gaining. It is laying hold of the love that has grasped and claimed us (Philippians 3:12).

Nevertheless, it takes a strong person, not a weak one, for this kind of letting go. Without letting go, without surrender, maturity does not come, and no goal is won. Letting go can take enormous strength and enormous love. Sometimes it takes all we have.

There are many in our midst who show us that only through letting go and trusting can we live lives of power. It is then that the one we trust most can live and love through us.

A great spiritual hero from the time of the Second World War, Dietrich Bonhoeffer, wrote in *The Cost of Discipleship*, "When Christ calls a man, he bids him come and die."[4] For Bonhoeffer, that was literal. It meant returning to Europe when he was safe in America, leaving a promising future at Union Theological Seminary to live in solidarity with the Confessing Church of Germany. It eventually meant execution at the hands of the Nazis.

Bonhoeffer let go of a future of great promise in order to give life to those whose hope was dying. His choice was the choice of the genuine disciple: to release anything that stands in the way of doing what Jesus would do if Jesus stood in our shoes—in our lives—in our situations; to let Christ take over our lives and, at any moment, to be ready to receive his directions.

This is not a theology of glory, of loving God for what we can get out of it. This is a theology of the cross. It is not to be confused with asceticism for the sake of becoming "holy," righteous, meritorious, or perfect before God. It is not self-denial with the mistaken conviction that we will thus gain heaven. A theology of the cross says that we follow the one who bore the cross. Where life is most cruel, most deprived, most empty, God comes, emptying God's self of love and life to fill our empty spaces. The theology of the cross invites us to do the same for others.

Heroes of the faith inspire us. But few of us think of ourselves as heroes. Of course, true heroes don't think of themselves that way either! They simply do what is needed, in the most loving way they can. They don't seem to be worried about their image.

"But," we may counter, "perhaps they are more strong than we are!" (Yet strength comes from using what we have.) "Perhaps they are buoyed up by an inspiring call from God." (But all of us are called.) "Perhaps they have not been wounded as much as we and their hearts are still strong and daring!" (But, as noted, the church has been built on the blood of such wounded martyrs.)

"We are tired," we may cry, "and we mourn what we have lost: the strength of younger, stronger bodies; the dear ones no longer with us; the opportunities that will never come again."

Yet something within us responds, "Mourning is necessary. It is recognition of our love and our need. And it is natural for the heart to bleed. But it is also natural for bleeding to stop and wounds to heal. Will you *allow* your healing?"

There comes a time to get on with living, to intentionally stop replaying old scenes remembered with feeling and living color in our brains, to stop bringing up old hurts in conversations, to forgive and ask for forgiveness so we can start again. There comes a time, by the grace of God, to discover a way to make stepping stones out of stumbling blocks and to look for a blessing in the pain.

This is the time when we are able to let go in order to let God take over. Luther's hero, Johannes Tauler, called it *Gelassenheit*: an abandonment of one's own self-centered will in order to receive God's love and leading in trust.[5] Regin Prenter, writing on Luther's understanding of the Holy Spirit's work, summarized it superbly: "Faith is the unconditional surrender . . . to God's sovereign grace."[6]

It is in the light of such trustful yielding that we need to look at some of the most harsh stories and directives of the Bible: the story of God's request that Abraham sacrifice his beloved son, Isaac; Jesus' directive to would-be disciples to "hate" and leave father and mother to follow him; the demand to "let the dead bury their dead"; and the requirement given the rich young ruler that he should sell everything he had in order to follow in God's path for him. One of Christ's most extreme and most inclusive statements may be Luke 14:33: "None of you can become my disciples if you do not give up all your possessions."

Jesus could not have been asking for callousness toward our loved ones. He taught that love for others was love for God. "As you did it to one of the least of these . . . , you did it to me" (Matthew 25:40). Love for God precedes and informs all our other loves. All of the above allusions say that nothing, no one, should stand in the way of our ultimate devotion to our creator. They are reminders of the First Commandment.

Furthermore, as a Middle Easterner speaking two thousand years ago, Jesus used "oriental hyperbole" naturally. He exaggerated to make a point. The point was the critical need for detachment from anything that would separate a person from his or her highest loyalty, the loyalty from which all others proceed.

Our greatest treasures can reveal the holy to us or distract us from it. The same thing can "veil" or "reveal" God depending on how we experience it. A dear child or a beloved parent, a cherished possession, an important professional opportunity: all can be seen as the Lord's gifts to us, God's means of touching us. When that is true, they are expressions of the holy and not something distracting us from God.[7]

THE SELF: IMPEDIMENT OR CHANNEL?

At the heart of Christian spirituality, indeed at the heart of all the great religions, is what I call the "s/S": self moving to become Self.[8]

Much spiritual writing of the past has referred to the "self" as something to be rejected and destroyed. This is the most negative way of interpreting "Deny yourself and follow me." Every living thing was created as a self and as such is loved by God, who "sees the sparrow fall." It is the sinful, self-preoccupied, self-centered self that Christ asks us to surrender. It is not the unique individuality that we each possess or our ability to respond and be responsible that is to be forsaken. It is a crime against God to put down the self that is made in God's image or to attempt to destroy it.

When our ordinary, immature, self-concerned being is offered to God and receives God's Spirit and consciously lives in God's presence, we move from self to Self. Our emptiness is filled with God's very life. The Self lives in God and God in the Self. "Abide in me as I abide in you" (John 15:4) summarizes the Self with a capital *S*. The Self is the person we are when we allow God to take over.

Many writers of the past and in all religions have written as though one can eventually grow to be a Self and remain at that "stage" for the rest of life. I must disagree. I have never met such a person. Life in the Holy Spirit is not static. We do not become perfect. We do not "arrive," never to sin again. We are always fluidly dependent upon the Spirit's life, offering itself to be our own.

Yet there is a process of transformation, and we *can* let go of the past, never to return. Paul's way of saying this is to refer to "the old man" and "the new creation." In 2 Corinthians 5:17 he writes: "If anyone is in Christ, there is a new creation: everything old has passed away; see, everything has become new!" Luther repeated Paul's terminology often. It is especially obvious in his treatise on "The Freedom of a Christian." There the ordinary self, bodily nature, "flesh" in bondage to sin, is called the "old," the "outer," the "carnal man." The reborn and regenerated individual is referred to as the "new," the "inner," and the "spiritual" person.[9]

Writing that deals with self-denial has too often led to destruction of body, health, and loving relationships through physical and social deprivation. But a healthy comprehension of self-denial deals not with denying ourselves pleasure or "things," but with letting go of the preoccupation with ourselves.

Of all the passages that expressed this to Luther, the following verses from Galatians 2:19-20 were among his favorites. These words are perhaps the best in all of the Bible to express the relationship between the self and Self, the old self-preoccupied person and "the new creation":

I have been crucified with Christ; and it is no longer I who live, but it is Christ who lives in me. And the life I now live in the flesh I live by faith in the Son of God, who loved me and gave himself for me.

Luther explains in his earlier lectures on Galatians, "Through faith Christ dwells in him and pours His grace into him through which . . . a man is governed, not by his own spirit but by Christ's.[10]

But the self is necessary. We do not exist or function without it. We meet God as a self, and that is life. We live as a self among selves. There is no community without the union of individual selves. We cannot even be a self unless it is in relation to other selves. Our faith is "our" faith, and our commitment or lack of it is our own. We die as a self, as Luther reminded us.[11] And we are raised as a beloved self.

All my young life I struggled with the question of "self." It seemed to me that I was told over and over not to "put myself forward," to instead "take the lowest place," to think of others as "better than" myself, and above all, not to "show off." I was also called to love God, to realize that my life belonged to God, and to offer myself for God's service. It was confusing! If I offered my own particular talents, which were weighted heavily in communications, I could not be hiding modestly in the background or taking the lowest place. A singer, speaker, or teacher has to be able to be in front of others. Doing any of those things with passion is not a self-effacing activity. It was easy to feel guilty even when doing my best for all the right reasons.

Finally after twenty years of confusion, I was given an understanding during my morning devotions. This is what I understood: the self is all we have to give to God. It is not God's mistake. All each of us has can be filled with God, but none of us will ever be all there is of God. The life and love of God surround and fill us. God is the larger. We are the smaller. We belong inside God. Then God can be inside of us. It can never be the other way around. Be at peace.

To me that meant that it was alright to be a performer. I was precious, loved. It was a good thing to be me. I could be true to myself and be who I was called to be simply by giving God my heart and all I was and had. The focus was not microscopically, analytically on me. It was on what God wanted to do through me. What a relief!

Faith exists when the self trusts, when it depends on the Holy Spirit to fill it, rule it, live and work through it. Through grace received by trusting love, not by effort, the self becomes a new creation. Sometimes we are flooded by the presence and power of God. It surely must be such times to which Luther referred when he said that Christ and we become one body.[12] It is at such times that we move from self to Self and the Holy Spirit fills us. Surely that is what God yearns for.

But few of us would feel that we are often one with God. In an older translation of Philippians 3:13-14, Paul speaks of the spiritual journey: "Not that I am perfect, but I press on." Why this perfectionist language? The answer is, he really is not speaking of perfectionism as we understand it. The Greek is difficult to translate, but it really means: "I am not yet full-grown. I am not yet mature. I am not yet qualified. I'm not ready!" But even so, "forgetting what lies behind and straining forward to what lies ahead, I press on toward the goal for the prize of the heavenly call of God in Christ Jesus."

What is that goal? For Paul, at that writing, it was to "know Christ and the power of his resurrection." It was also to pour himself out in sharing Christ. A writer named Étienne de Grellet is said to have written:

> I shall pass through this world but once. If, therefore, there be any kindness I can show, or any good thing I can do, let me do it now; let me not defer it or neglect it, for I shall not pass this way again.[13]

WAYS TO LIVE ATTACHMENT AND DETACHMENT

Is there a path of life that enables us to live for what matters? Is there an established pattern in which to live what we say we believe?

All too often the Christian answer has been a lopsided one. We go to extremes; we misunderstand what Scripture commands; or we misuse the guidance we have been given. Some of us are "so heavenly minded we are no earthly good." Others are so committed to healing the world that we have lost our connection to heaven. We burn ourselves out serving God because we do not drink enough from the simple well of receptive prayer. As each of these chapters reminds us, Christ asks us to love God with all of our heart, mind, soul, and strength and to love our neighbor as ourselves, even to love others as God loves us. Yet it is so easy to end up with exclusive, one-dimensional, either-or views rather than a balanced, inclusive approach embracing the "both-and" of faith and life, creed and discipleship, belief and trust, the active and passive.

Before the Reformation, God's call was thought to be only to full-time church vocations or to lives of prayer, discipline, and perhaps to doing good. Those who followed such a call usually chose a life of detachment or attachment, or some combination of the two. The purpose of detachment is to let go of anything that separates one from God. The path of attachment is understood as one in which all things good reveal God to us.

A life of detachment is one of release from distractions in order to attend to prayer and to God's goal for our lives. It is disconnecting ourselves from destructive influences in order to connect with what is creative and constructive. It is relinquishing position, power, possessions, and relationships when they get in the way of what God calls us to be.

A life of attachment, responsibility, and love emphasizes seeing God's presence revealed by people and nature, thoughts and things, that become for us means to know God and enable us to do God's will. It emphasizes habitual attachment to God by receptive prayer through which God guides us in the world. It is also attachment to the earth and its people, all of them created for each other.

We choose which way is best for us at which time. Common sense and devotion used together guide us. A mixture of the two approaches often seems best. The way of letting go says that unless destructive habits of mind and life are relinquished, they become stumbling blocks to loving God and others. The affirmative way says that where nature or people or art reveals God, showing God to be real and close, each of them can be a stepping stone toward knowing and sharing God.

The monastic approaches to the ways of detachment and attachment were, for Luther, ways that missed the mark. At least as a monk, he understood and applied them in a fashion with which he later disagreed. Luther saw both paths, of self-denial and of service used as "works," of letting go or doing good for the sake of gaining heaven. What seemed to be a good and righteous thing he had done for the wrong reason, and he believed others had also. He had, himself, used the paths of self-denial and service as a way of gaining heaven. He had done a good thing for the wrong reason. One time when he saw the difference clearly, he wrote: "They are wrong who make more of the act . . . than of the change of heart." It was, he said, "a glowing discovery."[14]

THE CHALLENGE

The self that is given is God's great treasure. It becomes a tool in the hand of God and an instrument of the Holy Spirit. If this is true, why are we not more effective instruments for God in this world, which so desperately needs to be touched by the holy and brought to true life? Why have we burned out and given up? Or why have we decided to "go along with the rest" and "make the best of it"?

Perhaps we have never known an intimate connection with God or we have lost it, so that life is not lived as prayer, as receptive and open to grace. But there are other reasons. The battle to be fought is *real*, and the adversaries are almost overwhelming. Many of us may have loved so hard and fought so long that we are exhausted. Or we have lost hope. We have been willing to suffer but not to be bold, to take risks, or to stand alone, and so we have lost our true power, which is God's power in us. Even if Christ was once born within us, Christ has not matured there, let alone gone out into the world of business, politics, ecology, and economics.

Of course, the wonder of Christ's birth within never happens to many people. For them, God is too far away or too far back in time, responsible for the fact of existence but completely uninvolved. Emmanuel (God with us), the incarnation, God's constant giving of the Holy Spirit—all seem unreal. If that is true for us, we can do little for God. Our disciplines of detachment or attachment will not help us. It is a serious matter. Dorothee Soelle, with Shirley A. Cloyes, writes in her book *To Work and to Love* that in theory, we believe in God, but in practice, our lives don't show it; we live as though we were atheists. She challenges us:

> Powerlessness is the nonbeliever's perspective. "There's nothing we can do about it" is the voice of practical atheism. In the United States there exists a strange combination of theoretical theism and practical atheism. People believe in some supreme being "up there," but this heavenly being does not change anything here, neither in my heart, nor in my community, nor in the world.[15]

If Christ is born in our hearts, will the world ever feel it? Will government and business, our beloved earth or our disenfranchised masses be affected? We cannot answer that we are not good enough or are not schooled enough or are not recognized. We can only begin where we are.

The Christ who calls us from the depths of our being, who commissions us to witness to what we know in our hearts, is the one who brings life abundant, not only to us but through us, the church and its members. Each of us chooses to be part of this world's problems or its solutions, a connection or disconnection from God's love, a spark fed by the fire of God's Spirit or one that flies from the fire and dies alone.

Jesus was a realist. "In the world you face persecution," he stated, "but take courage; I have conquered the world" (John 16:33).

Furthermore, we have a promise: "You will receive power when the Holy Spirit has come upon you" (Acts 1:8). The choice is up to us. To all those who receive him, who believe in his name, Christ still gives "the power to become the children of God" (John 1:12) and, with this inheritance, his grace to love to life the earth and all its people.

ABIDING IN GOD'S HEART

LIFE AS PRAYER

Abiding is coming home to stay, to stay in the place where we were born, the heart of God in which we were conceived. Abiding is returning to live in the place where we truly belong—where we are nourished, at peace, and secure. Yet, in one way or another, all of us leave "home," just as we all leave the womb. The leaving and the returning seem to be part of the life journey. In all probability, they are necessary, a means to recognize where we belong and to whom. Like Adam and Eve, we seek for something that will satisfy us completely, even though we have always lived in the presence of God. We only seem to recognize what matters most when desires and distractions show us, by contrast, what is truly our greatest need and deepest love.

Folktales across the world have long told the story. They point out the pervasive quest for riches, the search for "the pot of gold," the quest for the Grail, the supreme treasure. And the stories end with the exhausted but wiser seeker returning home to discover there what she had searched the world to find. The journey itself has taught the traveler to recognize, to appreciate, and to be grateful for what matters most—and is so surprisingly close—and then to *cling* to it.

We discover, wherever we go that it is important to hold onto home in our hearts, for there, Jesus tells us, God longs to dwell (John 14:23). Perhaps by grace we will discover that wherever we are, we can be at home, for home is the presence of God, and there we can "abide."

There is a longing in every one, a longing for something missing, a longing for completion, a longing for fulfillment. It motivates most of the things we do. We call it by many names and try to satisfy it in countless ways. In the end, we may discover the one thing that matters most and learn that everything else matters because of it. It is the realization of which Augustine wrote at the beginning of his *Confessions*: "Our hearts are restless until they rest in thee."

Jesus spoke of this personal need for the one he called "the Father." But the devil tempted him with all kinds of hunger: the hunger for food to survive, the hunger for temporal power over others, and the impulse to "prove" God's power in his life. His reply to the tempter was clear: "One does not live by bread alone, but by every word that comes from the mouth of God" (Matthew 4:4). To his disciples, he said, "I have food to eat that you do not know about" (John 4:32).

When we are hungry, we need something we do not have. We reach out for something more. The miracle is that all hungers can lead us to God. Or they can lead us away.

The good and beautiful reveal the holy. And they can distract from it. The ugly and warped can destroy us. Or they can impel us to find our strength in God.

What is the difference between a stumbling block and a stepping-stone? Could it be our grounding in God, our connectedness to God and to each other as the people of God?

In his last, never-to-be-forgotten evening with his friends, Jesus did what so many do when they know they are about to die. He spoke of what mattered most. He told his friends that he loved them. He asked that they take care of each other for his sake. Then he added something vitally important: "Abide in me as I abide in you. . . . Apart from me you can do nothing" (John 15:4-5). What did he mean?

Abiding is dwelling, living in God: a constant connection, a continuing communion based on complete trust. Jesus was going away bodily, but his Spirit would remain, abiding with those he loved. He invited his followers to reciprocate, to depend on him and on the one who sent him.

Luther called it being "cemented" to God. Underhill called it "adhering." Ancient Jews referred to it as "clinging." The Eastern Orthodox see it as awareness or "watchfulness." Buddhists name it "mindfulness." Muslims urge constant, faithful, "remembering." Many people worldwide see it as a state of "resting in the Lord," an experience of great peace. Abiding can be waiting, with patience. But it can also be dogged trust in the midst of active struggle, confusion, and pain.

When Paul said to "pray without ceasing" (1 Thessalonians 5:17), he was describing abiding. Prayer is connecting to God, communion with God, a state of openness to God's guidance and love. Prayer is not only a way of worship, but a way of life: life lived in awareness that we dwell in the perpetual presence of God. Abiding is living in trust, and that way of life is prayer.

Luther once stated that "the whole life of the new people . . . is nothing else but prayer."[1] He taught that "praying should continue in the heart almost without interruption" in that all we do is used to glorify God and bring in the kingdom.[2] When preaching he said, "Christians are bound to pray without ceasing, if not with the lips, . . . yet with the heart."[3] And he spoke of our unvoiced longings and wishes as prayers. In giving his barber "A Simple Way to Pray," he wrote, "There are works that are as good as or better than a prayer . . . . All the works of believers are prayers." Then he quoted an old proverb: "The faithful worker offers a double prayer." Yes, true prayer comes from the heart, but it can be expressed through words or work: through one's life.[4]

There is a danger, however, in thinking of work as prayer. Many of us can get so caught up in work that we forget to root it in the guidance of God. Work cannot be prayer without that indispensable relationship, and that requires remembering whose work it is.

Neglecting prayer is serious. It severs the connection between ourselves and the Savior.[5] In *Life Together*, Dietrich Bonhoeffer insists that an hour set aside daily for meditation on scripture, prayer, and intercession is not only a duty but a need. He says strongly, "We have a right to this time, even prior to the claims of other people. . . . For the pastor it is an indispensable duty and his whole ministry will depend upon it."[6]

WATCHING JESUS ABIDE

Jesus knew how important his final admonition to his disciples was, because nothing had been more important to him than abiding. To consciously "abide" in the presence of the one he called his Father was the only way he could fulfill his mission, to be who he was: the Christ. "I have not spoken on my own," he claimed. "The Father who has sent me has himself given me a commandment about what to say and what to speak" (John 12:49). "The Father who dwells in me does his works" (John 14:10). "I have come . . . to do . . . the will of him who sent me" (John 6:38).

The only way that Jesus knew to fulfill his purpose on earth was to stay connected with the one whose will it was. Prayer was the essence of his life. We learn how to abide by watching Jesus.

Jesus was also abiding, says Olé Hallesby, when he "went apart" before the most demanding challenges of his lifetime: when deciding upon his earthly mission, before choosing his disciples, when avoiding those who would make him king, and when preparing for his trial and crucifixion.[7] That last time, we are told, he "sweat blood" in his abiding. It was not joyous or peaceful. The night was one of agony. Yet he was able to survive it and walk even further into pain because he knew he was not alone.

For us, too, abiding can be the most blessed, peaceful, and grace-filled experience one can have. It can also be the most intense spiritual struggle possible: hanging on to God in spite of fear, confusion, and deep conflicting desires. Abiding seems to happen most naturally in the extremes of peace or pain or challenge.

Abiding in a Totalitarian State

Much as I wish it were not true, abiding is not constant in my life. Yet there are hundreds of cases where, by opening my heart to the one who is always hanging on to me, wonderful, graced things have happened, as they have, no doubt, for many of you.

Adding together the five trips we have made, my husband and I have spent more than a year in the former Soviet Union, where he was invited as an exchange scientist. Our early trips were my first and most intense long-term experiences of prayer-without-ceasing, of real abiding. They occurred because of the challenges under which we lived.

Those were the days when people disappeared from Moscow's streets. An American newspaper man with whom I had eaten lunch was imprisoned on a trumped-up charge shortly after we arrived. My husband, Ed, and I each walked the streets alone, always presuming that we might be followed. We knew our phone was bugged and had every reason to assume our rooms were as well. We took it for granted that our possessions would be searched at any time. We were advised that government-employed maids and guides, even if they were our friends, were expected to report on our activities daily.

One visitor wrote messages. We read them silently. Then they were torn into little pieces and flushed down the drain. We remembered that incident when my husband saw militiamen opening a manhole and carefully looking through the contents of the drain directly across the street.

One person who was invited to some of my concerts was intensively interrogated twice by the KGB because he was suspected as a dissident. During the questioning, he thought more than once that he might have a heart attack.

A friend who arranged some of my concerts was always absent when I sang Menotti's "Magda's Aria," a heart-wrenching aria about the wife of a freedom fighter trying to get official papers to leave a totalitarian state. Yet I had officially presented all my music ahead of time and, amazingly, it had all been cleared.

I shall never forget the small, frightened little voice of a friend singing to me in the back seat of a car so that no one else could hear: "We shall overcome . . . someday!" Nor will I cease to remember the day I spoke for all the Methodist ministers of the Soviet bloc countries in Talinn, Estonia, on the subject of "Receptive Prayer," only to learn, as I stood to speak, that the vice-chairman of the Communist Party of Estonia was in my audience.

Before we left that weekend of encounter, I sang a concert for those pastors and a church crammed to the windowsills with people. Although I was a woman, because I was "explaining" my music, I was allowed to speak. The theme of my words and songs was the children of Israel looking forward to the promised land, always knowing that God walked with them and before them.

My husband and I shared a meal with pastors who had been imprisoned for years in concentration camps after World War II. When asked what they needed, their most urgent request was not for money, goods, schooling, or even political favors. It was for prayer. "Please don't forget us!" was their plea. I wish you could have seen the urgency in their eyes. Since then I have not only prayed for them but for the forgotten all around the world. Sometimes I concentrate on only one unknown, unnamed individual, lost from all those who love him. Who has any idea of the depths of isolation into which God's love can penetrate?

Every moment, we were reminded of where we were and why. In such an atmosphere, is it any wonder that one could easily live with an unceasing sense of the presence of God? We *had* to stay connected to our Source for guidance and for peace.

Abiding may well be the most pervasive, inclusive, and difficult thing for us to learn to do in our lives, but it can be greatly facilitated by extreme challenge. For then we must make a decision. We must choose between fear and hopelessness or trust. If the choice is trust, God's response can be amazing. In some ways, those days in Russia were easier than facing normal life in America. Our mission was very clear, and our sustenance was constant.

"OUR" PRAYER BEGINS WITH GOD

Prayer is not primarily something we do by our own effort. It is useless to pray in order to manipulate the Almighty or to demonstrate that we are good. Prayer that is done to convince God we are worthy of salvation or anything else is, for Luther, a "work."

"For him," says the Catholic scholar Jared Wicks, S.J., "the whole of the Christian life is subsumed under the heart's yearning for God's interior work of renewal." In this vein Luther wrote that prayer is "the seeking and begging by the yearning of the heart, the voice of the mouth, and the labor of the body."[8] The "yearning of the heart" is really what is most important. Spiritual giants have always told us that prayer is fundamentally a desire to be with God, the essence of abiding. It is our deepest need.

This yearning is implanted by the Holy Spirit. In commenting on John 14:13-14, Luther said, "The presence of the Spirit of grace grants us the privilege and creates in us the ability, nay, the necessity, to begin to pray."[9]

If that is true, then prayer is not even our own idea. Just as "we love God because God loves us," Luther says that we can pray because God has made us able to respond. God calls us through the silent voice of our hunger, saying, "Come, let me love you that you may love me, too."

Perhaps, like Moses or Elijah, we begin by seeking after God, arduously climbing up the mountain of prayer, only to realize that God has planted our yearning for the mountaintop within us. Tillich tells us that even to "miss" God, to feel that God is absent, is a reminder by the real and very present God of the one who seems to be gone.[10] Our search for God is really God's idea, and God has been waiting for us to hear the call wherever we may be. Prayer is, first of all, God's initiative. Then it becomes our answer to God's pervasive call.

How blessed it is to know that the Spirit prays in us wordlessly, as Romans 8:26-27 has indicated: "We do not know how to pray as we ought, but that very Spirit intercedes with sighs too deep for words. And God, who searches the heart, knows what is the mind of the Spirit." Thus prayer begins with the presence of God calling to us, even communicating for us, from the very center of our beings. When we are in prayer, we are participating in something God has already started.

God speaks to us and for us at our deepest level, deeper than our surface consciousness. This is one reason that sacraments and symbols, nature and art communicate to us in a way that requires no words or thought in response. This is why adoration is most often wordless. There are many people who are "not good with words" who pray a great deal. They may not even realize they are praying. They have allowed themselves to be touched by God. They receive, and they respond by the way they live.

God is at home in us at this most basic, fundamental, simple level. There prayer begins before it is thought or spoken, sung or played on an instrument, cried, sighed, or lived. Ann Ulanov of Union Theological Seminary calls prayer at this level "primary speech."[11] It is not uttered aloud. Such speech begins with the sighs of the Holy Spirit within us.

Trying to explain this intimacy of the Holy Spirit in us, Harry Emerson Fosdick writes in *The Meaning of Prayer*: "God is constantly compelled to minister his blessing to us through our own capacities to receive and appropriate":

> During a dry season in the New Hebrides, John G. Paton, the missionary, awakened the derision of the natives by digging for water. They said water always came down from heaven, not up through the earth. But Paton revealed a larger truth than they had seen before by discovering to them that heaven could give them water through their own land. So [people] insist on waiting for God to send them blessing in some super-normal way,

when all the while he is giving them abundant supply if they would only learn to retreat into the fertile places of their own spirits, where, as Jesus said, the wells of living waters seek to rise. We need to learn Eckhart's lesson, "God is nearer to me than I am to myself; he is just as near to wood and stone, but they do not know it."[12]

THE NATURALNESS OF PRAYER

Yes, Meister Eckhart was surely right: "God is nearer to me than I am to myself." There is no need to memorize someone else's words or use a prescribed format to communicate with the one whom we call "Father" or "Mother-Father God." We do not depend on the written words of others to speak to our family, and the one to whom we pray is even closer.

We can simply "be" (abide) with this one who loves us so, just as we are with friends and family whom we love. Then, if we feel like talking, we can simply say what is in our hearts. We can be more honest with God, who already knows our depths, than we are with anyone else or even ourselves. And it is in being honest before the unconditional love of God that we gain the courage to know the truth about ourselves. If we are open and honest with God, God will teach us how to pray.

Luther understood this. He preached a sermon on Romans 12:7-16 in which he said:

> Out of a book you will never pray anything good. To be sure, you may read from the book and learn how and what you should pray, and you may kindle your devotion; but a prayer must come from the heart spontaneously, without any prepared and prescribed words; it must speak its own language according to the fervor of the heart.[13]

Then, when teaching the Lord's Prayer to laity, Luther commented, ending with sharp humor:

> The essence and the nature of prayer are nothing else than the raising of the soul or heart to God. But if the nature and the art of prayer consist in the raising of the heart, it follows that everything which is not a lifting up of the heart is not prayer. Therefore singing, speaking, and piping, when not accompanied by the rising of the heart to God, are prayers as much as

the scarecrows in the garden are men. The essence is not there, but only the appearance and the name.[14]

STEPS IN PRAYER:
REMEMBERING, RETURNING, AND RESTING

Since we were children some of us have heard, memorized, and repeated, "Remember the Sabbath day and keep it holy." We need to remember the Sabbath, not for God's sake, but for our own. It is true that "in returning and rest you shall be saved; in quietness and in trust shall be your strength" (Isaiah 30:15). For those in the helping professions and for the many who today are supposed to do the work of two or three people, this is imperative. Without "returning and rest," without "refueling," our vessels will soon be empty, and we will begin to forget that "our" ministry is really God's. We need the Sabbath day and many little Sabbaths in between.

My beloved mother used to look at me quite seriously when I was working too hard and admonish, "Grace Mary, a dry sponge cannot give any water!" It is not our own reserves that are endless but God's. Only what we have received will give us life. Only what we have received can we give away. We cannot live if we do not receive.

The receiving begins by remembering and returning. Jesus' words in the Eucharist are "Do this in remembrance of me." There is no religious community without remembering the creative and saving work of God. And if God is forgotten, nothing has its true meaning. That is why we have prayer before meals and before and after sleeping. That is why we have regular Sunday worship. That is why there are up to seven canonical hours for prayer in Christian monasteries, and why Muslims pray toward Mecca five times a day. That is the reason for religions across the world celebrating yearly holidays.

In all religious societies, artists help people to return to the divine by creating reminders of God in picture, song, and dance, through architecture and symbol. The wonder is that what begins by simply reminding us goes on to put us in touch with the holy. The same thing happens when we memorize precious life-giving words that have inspired us and given us strength in the past. Remembering them, experiencing them later, may give comfort or hope or even keep us sane. But we will never notice any of these if we do not "draw apart" form the noise, confusion, fragmentation, and pressure that pervade the world in which we live.

We cannot be mindful of God, pay attention to Christ's call, or be watchful of the Spirit's leading unless we remember and return to the still center of life. In some ways, a relationship with God is no different from human love or friendship. People contemplating divorce often say, "We just grew apart." And it is absolutely true. If we want to grow close, the first rule to follow is to make arrangements to be together often. Human relationships are impossible without it. So is our relationship with God, and prayer is the means of meeting.[15] We remember. Because we remember, we return. And when we have returned, we can rest.

There is no replacement for conscious rest in God's presence, a rest in which we can place all our care on God's shoulders. Scripture and song have described it so well: "Come to me, all you that are weary and are carrying heavy burdens, and I will give you rest" (Matthew 11:28). It is in that kind of rest that we can be healed. And it is with prayer, which is resting in God, that we can minister best to the sick and dying. (My book *Receptive Prayer* describes ways to do this.)

But healing takes time, just as resting does. And good things distract us from prayer. Where can we find the time for prayer? There is no extra time. Prayer must be put where something else would be. Something else will have to go.

"O Lord!" we cry. "What? When? How?" God answers simply: "Where your treasure is, there your heart will be also" (Matthew 6:21). "You have asked me to help you, to guide you, to heal, and to inspire. But I am already here. It is you who need to turn your attention."

A beloved older friend once gave me a metaphor to hang on to. "Be like the camel," she said. "You have a long distance to go, and the burdens you carry are heavy. But you can put them down for awhile to rest. When you are refreshed, you can pick them up again. They will still be there if you want them." Of course, what often happens is that through prayer we decide to carry something else upon our hearts, or we learn a better way to bear our burdens.

SILENCE, COMMUNITY, AND SOLITUDE

"Be still, and know that I am God" (Psalm 46:10). Silence, mystery, and majesty seem to belong together. Only in silence can we seem to touch the limitless and awesome abyss of God, the very depths of God's being from which all of God's riches, all of God's outpouring love proceeds. Out of silence comes the voice of God.

There is a contemplative community in the inner city of Detroit that calls itself The Friends of Silence. On all their communications is a caption that reads "Is there enough Silence for the Word to be heard?"[16]

God's message is preached and sung exultantly, but it is not always heard in words. There are many forms of art, nature, and compassion that speak for God. All of them have proceeded from the storehouse of silence that contains everything that exists. The hymn "Let All Mortal Flesh Keep Silence" is a magnificent vehicle to experience this very truth.

Remember Elijah upon the mountaintop? Wanting to die, he nevertheless made his way to Mount Horeb. There he waited, watched, and listened through earthquake, wind, and fire, straining for a word from God. When the fury was finished, the word finally came as a barely audible voice, a thin whisper (1 Kings 19:12).[17] That day, God's word could be heard only in the most profound silence.

In the silence we are loved. In the silence we are led. In the silence we may understand, not necessarily with the brain, but with the heart. In silence there is healing. And in silence we find peace. God speaks through silence, calls to us in our hearts, and enlightens our understanding. Our institutions, the sacraments, and the sacred written Word cannot confine the Living Word. Nor can we decide for God the limits within which God will speak. We know only that the Spirit deals with us where we are, through a natural world and natural means when we are simple enough to hear and see. Evelyn Underhill once commented, "Our deepest contacts with God are so gentle because they are all we can bear. We need quiet to experience them."[18]

Few things are as profound as sharing silence with a worshiping community. The silence is often greater than the deepest silence in solitude, almost as though the depth has been multiplied. Together every mind and heart are offered, aware of the real presence of the holy. In such a setting we can understand how many souls can be as one or "gathered," as the Quakers say. We can experience how, in Christ, there is no separation. Such moments transform lives. People around us become special, for we share what really matters with them. It is treasured time. There are many of us who would appreciate it deeply if the time before a worship service were considered such a sacred, silent time. We need it desperately. The church narthex is the natural place for conversation with each other. The church nave is probably the only place we know that is consecrated for worship.

A congregation can be more than a friendly community. It can be a fellowship alive with the Holy Spirit, a fellowship in which there is no necessity to fill every moment with talk. Indeed, as in a deep love between two people, there are times when to talk would spoil it all. As a congregation sits in quietness, the organist's music can become what is intended: a prayer without words, to center us on why we are present. Silence can be savored. It is its own prayer.

Dietrich Bonhoeffer's words on silence, community, and solitude in *Life Together* teach how silence allows us to receive and how "right speech comes out of silence, and right silence comes out of speech." Ponder his words, applying them to a Sunday worship service as well as to private devotions:

> Silence is the simple stillness of the individual under the Word of God. We are silent before hearing the Word because our thoughts are already directed to the Word, as a child is quiet when he enters his father's room. We are silent after hearing the Word because the Word is still speaking and dwelling within us. We keep silence solely for the sake of the Word, . . . to honor and receive it.[19]

With these words, Bonhoeffer moves from writing about silence in the congregation to personal silent meditation. His words are specifically about *lectio divina*, the prayerful reading of Scripture.[20]

RECEPTIVE PRAYER

In Revelation 3:20 we read God's ageless invitation: "Listen! I am standing at the door, knocking; if you hear my voice and open the door, I will come in to you and eat with you." Luther put it in a similar way, "This is Christ the Lord, for whom you have yearned and sighed. He is standing before your door. . . . Receive your Lord, and accept Him!"[21] Some years earlier, preaching about Ephesians 6:18, he said, "He wants you to open your bosom that he may give to you. [And you will] receive more and more, the longer you hold open your sack."[22]

Our bottomless inner spaces know what we need. Nothing but our Lord's love can satisfy. So we must stop and do nothing except let God love us. We discover that is prayer.

God calls us to an embrace, and in that embrace we find profound rest. We experience our deepest trust. It is life-giving. It matters more than anything else. No wonder that in prayer we can "come to ourselves" as did another prodigal child. It is there that we know what we need and where we belong. We remember Psalm 37: "Be still before the Lord, and wait patiently for him"; "trust in the Lord, . . . and he will give you the desires of your heart." But what is our heart's desire, the desire beyond all others? For most of us it is a yearning to be loved, to be deeply cherished. And it is also a longing to give: to share love and joy, to give life!

Prayer is a way of discovering that we are loved, that we are cherished, and that we have a well of love to share. Some prayers can simply be loving God and letting God love us. Others can be loving others with God's love.

Imagine Jesus praying. Surely he laid himself bare to the one he called "Father." He opened his heart and was awake to guidance given. We can't imagine him merely listing his needs and wants—as we are prone to—saying Amen, and turning away as if the prayer were over!

We can imagine Jesus' prayer as listening and communing with his Father, allowing the Father to live, inspire, strengthen, and guide him. Our prayers can be that simple and profound, too. The essence of prayer is savoring God's presence, drinking it in as desert plants drink in the water of life, as trees absorb the sunshine, as all living things breathe in. God's Spirit is the food we need. Thus a "breath prayer" is the most natural prayer of all and one of the simplest. We cannot live without breathing; we cannot live without God. Breathing is constant and usually unconscious; God is constant, frequently unperceived.

Thus to breathe in consciously and to simultaneously receive God's Spirit and love is life-giving. In breathing out, we can let go of anything that stands in the way of God's love: pain, anxiety, tension, or sadness. This, too, is the time for offering up our inadequacies, our sin, the garbage that clogs our lifeline. Breathing out can also become our self-offering to God in response to God's self-offering to us. Eventually, after all concern for self or others has been relinquished, our prayer may become only the breathing in and out of God's love. Receptive prayer receives grace, and grace heals us and others.

It is then that we can most effectively include others for whom we pray. We offer them to God. We think of the holy breath breathed into their lungs as it was breathed into Adam's. We picture them as serene, surrendered, and receptive. We see them as being healed, becoming joyous, free, and whole.

Before concluding prayer, it is important to ask God a question: "What do you want me to do for you? How can my normal duties become an expression of your love? Whom do you want me to notice?" The life of prayer is given not to help us to accomplish what may be our shortsighted or self-centered will but to allow us to discover and claim God's will for our own. When such trustful resting in the Lord is ended and we find ourselves refreshed, we can pause to remember and savor what was important in the time just past, to write it down in our spiritual journals, and to say, "Thank you, Lord."[23] (Assistance in learning how to pray in this receptive, contemplative manner is given in chapters 2 and 3 of *Receptive Prayer*.)

PRAYER AS A SACRAMENT

The Apology to the Augsburg Confession asks, "If we should list as sacraments all the things that have God's command and a promise connected to them, then why not prayer, which can most truly be called a sacrament?"[24]

Communion itself is surely the most perfect model of prayer. Here, in the living presence of God, the life of God is given. "This is my body, broken for you." "Eat, that you may live." "This is my blood, shed for you. Drink of it, all of you." Christ is saying, "Receive what I have lived and died to give."

Then God's gift is given, and we who have waited stretch out our upturned hands to receive the bread and wine. We swallow them and receive them into our bodies, where they become part of blood and nerves and sinews.

This surely is the very heart of prayer: to yield in order to offer our minds, ourselves, our lives to grace that has already called us.

Then, by that grace, to be spoken to and given to, and finally, also by grace, to receive in faith.

The word outwardly spoken and inwardly heard in the heart—the promised Presence given and received—these surely are the essence of what true prayer is and the heart of what Jesus called "abiding." Throughout our days, we offer back to the one who has invited and welcomed us our own invitation and welcome, indeed our plea, as did the apostles on the road to Emmaus: "Abide with us, our Savior" (Luke 24:29 KJV)!

THE SUFFERING HEART

WHERE IS GOD WHEN WE SUFFER?

It was January of 1991. The Gulf War had recently begun. That morning I was teaching a university course in theology, looking into the eyes of two fresh-faced ROTC students who sat directly in front of me. They looked so young, so unaware of the terrible pain they might soon have to bear. Yet we all realized that they might be facing their first battlefield before the semester ended.

Our subjects that week were "How Do We Know God Is Real?" and "If God Is Real, So What?" Just ten minutes after we had begun, a student interrupted, blurting out, "Dr. Brame, when is God going to step in and stop this war?"

I was taken aback. But the urgency in her voice told me my response would be important. I answered as simply and quietly as I could, "Do you think God will do that? Did God start the war?"

It happened again this week, and it happened the week before. A young mother painfully asked, "Why does God take little babies?" And a young man, a self-confessed cynic, challenged, "Did God make Eden's serpent evil?" Perhaps the hardest question to hear came from a young Jewish woman: "If there is a God, why does he hate us so much?"

It is wonderful to teach a required course in religion! It means that people who would never choose to think about God must deal with questions of ultimate importance, life-and-death issues, values that will give a goal and a frame for their lives or at least will have to be consciously dismissed rather than unconsciously ignored for a lifetime. It also means that religion is less likely to be treated as a hallowed subject, less likely to be a sham. If their honesty is valued, those who believe little or nothing may point up the real issues and become some of the most valuable members of the class.

Longtime Christians are not always so honest with themselves. My friend's husband was killed by a drunk driver who ran a red light at nine o'clock in the morning. A warm and compassionate man, he was on his way to shower life-giving love to children in the slums. Someone said, intending to help, "He was so good! God needed him in heaven."

Those words were almost too much to bear! Was it God's "plan" that the other driver be drunk, that he disobey the law, that he kill a very special person whose life was given to making the world a better place? Was God responsible, or was that drunken man? Did "God make him do it," or was it a senseless, irresponsible act that didn't have to happen?

Where is God when tragedy occurs? Why doesn't God intervene? Doesn't God control the world?

No, I don't think so. I don't think God controls us or nature or history. If that were true, faith would be unnecessary. There would be no need for prayer or listening for God's guidance. We would not be asked to follow Christ. Everything would be decided by a greater authority. There would be no need for the commandments or Jesus' teaching. In fact, if God controlled the world, why wouldn't God make everyone good and take them all to heaven?"

Life is so important, so precious, that we cannot bear to think that tragedy could be senseless, useless, without meaning. For some, it is frightening to think that nothing, no one, is controlling what happens. On the other hand, it is breathtaking to realize that all of us are granted the awesome freedom to give life or destroy it—every day of our existence. Most of us do both.

I have spent too much of my life hearing Christian friends say resignedly: "It must be God's will." "God had a reason for it." "God meant it for good." "God is testing me." Words like this help some of us accept what is otherwise unacceptable so that we can go on. But they also confuse, anger, and turn others away from religion. To these individuals, such a God seems fickle, not faithful; hateful, not holy.

What kind of a God do we believe in? If God is good, why is there evil and suffering? Buddhism and Hinduism answer: "Because of our desire," because of our greed. And a Christian might respond: "Isn't that the same as self-centeredness? Isn't that what Luther meant by being 'curved in on oneself?'"Islam often says: "What happens is the will of God." But it also insists that to forget God is the worst of all sin and has dire consequences.

One pervasive understanding in the Judeo-Christian tradition is that suffering is a result of sin, the retribution of a just God, beginning with the expulsion from the Garden of Eden. Calvin accepted this, and wrote as much in *Forms of Prayer for the Church*: "Scriptures teach us that Pestilence, War, and other calamities of this kind are chastisements of God, which he inflicts on our sins."[1]

SUFFERING FOR OUR FAITH

Numerous sections of Hebrew scripture say that the righteous, those who have kept the Law, will not suffer (although some of Israel's anointed prophets suffered mightily).[2] But it is obvious that good people do suffer. The primary and most extreme example is Jesus. During the Last Supper, he stated very clearly, "In the world you face persecution" (John 16:33). He warned that to follow him might lead not to prosperity but to death: "Then they will hand you over to be tortured and will put you to death, and you will be hated by all nations because of my name" (Matthew 24:9). He even stated that those "righteous ones" who would destroy his followers would think that they were doing God a favor (John 16:2-4)!

Strangely enough, religion itself is the cause of much suffering. Religious superiority assumes it is the sole possessor, guardian, and defender of eternal truth. The idea that "error has no rights" has been deeply ingrained in fundamentalist radicals in every religion in history. It has been the conviction behind imprisonment, torture, execution, and all "religious" wars (which sometimes should be known as wars that use religion as an excuse).

Arrogant religiosity has now turned mightily against Christianity. Reporting on Nina Shea's book *In the Lion's Den*, the *Wall Street Journal* reported that "few Americans know that Christians today are the most persecuted religious group in the world and that persecution is intensifying."[3]

In the late twentieth century, one million non-Muslims were starved, abducted, or killed by their own government in the Sudan. Thousands of Christians were sold as slaves. Torture, imprisonment, rape, kidnapping, and forced conversions of children, execution, crucifixion, and even flaying (skinning alive) have been reported as inflicted upon Christians in that country.[4]

Persecution is also waged by those whose religion is secularism. Secularism is no longer simply life without God. It has become the disavowal of God. Lifestyles and values of any kind are allowed, even taught in schools, so long as they ignore the holy. In spite of the carefully crafted First Amendment to the Constitution, which provides that "Congress shall pass no law respecting an establishment of religion or *prohibiting the free exercise thereof*" (emphasis added), militant secularism infringes on citizens' freedom to express religious belief publicly. But antireligious values are often given unrestricted liberty.

Bit by bit, with the help of naive good people who do not realize what is happening, secularism is forcing Christianity into a ghetto of "privacy" where it is losing its social force. I cannot help but ask, when the water has all "run down the drain," slowly and imperceptibly to many—when religion has become completely private or, at the most, the province of churches alone—will we wonder how it happened?

Most Western Christians are unprepared for persecution. Many are convinced of the ancient Hebrew view that a righteous life should bring blessing. But they have missed Christ's teaching to "take up your cross and follow me," that "those who want to save their life will lose it" (Mark 8:34-35). Thus there are many good people who are bitter and disappointed in a God to whom they have given everything, a God who some sections of the Old Testament said would repay them in happiness and prosperity.

Luther's own life taught him otherwise. As we have noted, he often spoke of his suffering as *Anfechtung*, translated variously as trials, temptations, assault by the devil, panic, despair, doubt, and desolation. He believed that a Christian is constantly assailed by such challenges. Certainly it was frequently his own experience.[5] In a letter of 1516 he wrote, "The cross of Christ is distributed through the whole world, and to everybody inevitably comes his portion of it. Do you, therefore, not cast it aside, but rather take it up as a holy relic." At other times he stated, "If Christ wore a crown of thorns, we should not expect people to place wreaths and roses on our heads." "He who does not bear his cross is no Christian, for he is not like his Master, Christ." But he was cautionary as well. He insisted that no one "search" for crosses, advising, "We are neither to seek the cross nor to flee from it."[6]

Cross-bearing for Luther is confined to suffering for the sake of Christ and the gospel. He teaches that people do not become martyrs because they suffer; they become martyrs when they suffer *for the right*. "Every Christian is called Christophorus, that is, a Christ-bearer." And to bear Christ is to live as Christ would live in our place and time.[7]

It is not "ordained" by God that those who love must suffer. It is simply inevitable that in truly loving, we sometimes will. If we care about the people begging on our streets or about those born into ignorance or AIDS; if we care about victims (and perpetrators) of crime; about people caught in compulsions; about lives destroyed by famine, poverty, and genocide; about loved ones with lifelong daily pain—then we will suffer. It is impossible to avoid it.

Theologian Dorothee Soelle lived in Germany during the agony of the Holocaust. She points out that suffering may be an inevitable consequence of love. Using the crucifixion as an example, she says that we who live for others will suffer because we bear each other's pain. And further, in giving life to others, some of our own life is bound to be offered up. Quoting the Russian poet, Konstantin Simonov, she writes, "There is no alien sorrow."[8] Who does not know of lives that have been given up completely for the sake of love? Which of us has not suffered for another?

OTHER CAUSES OF SUFFERING

To blame God as the direct instigator of everything that ever happens is to ignore that we are participants in history and bear much responsibility for ourselves and each other. E. Stanley Jones in his compassionate book *Christ and Human Suffering* has named three clear reasons for suffering:

- We can inherit physical suffering through our genes.
- We can be influenced or victimized by sick people and a sick society.
- We ourselves can make choices that lead to suffering of ourselves or others.[9]

It is the inevitable consequence of free will.

There are scores of books published today that, in an effort to help people recognize the nonphysical causes of sickness and pain, point to underlying spiritual and psychological factors. These books are extremely valuable, because we are psychosomatic beings, creatures of body and psyche, both of which affect the other in ways of which we are barely aware. But we need to be cautious of advice that says that if we were psychologically healthy or spiritually "right with God," "no plague could come near (our) dwelling," no germ could get a foothold, and no inherited weaknesses could be manifested.

On the other hand, bodies and minds can be spiritually healed even when the cause of suffering may not be spiritual. Victims of accidents can testify to that. We need to object to statements that indicate that the only cause of physical suffering is spiritual or psychological. We do not know and cannot prove that this is a fact, so we should not say so. I have seen suffering people accept this with the result that their agony increased. Sensitive people realize their imperfections and may spend years scouring their souls, dredging up garbage that does not need to be examined again and again and getting sicker because of it. "Facing our tigers" is one of the most important things we do, but there comes a time to let go of the past and give it all to God.

There are other causes for suffering. We like to think that we live in a predictable, cause-and-effect world. But my scientist husband often reminds me that in spite of the "laws" of nature, in spite of a cosmos whose very name means "order," there is randomness. Some things coincide that are not part of a pattern (at least any pattern of which we now know). Because of lack of information, people discover themselves at the wrong place at the wrong time, although it is no one's "fault." Randomness is not only a factor in suffering, however. It also can bring surprising and valuable gifts.

There are multitudes of people who simply do not know that God exists. They have never experienced God's creative and life-giving Spirit. Fresh out of college, I took several jobs that would enable me to "see another side of life." And I did. Daily I worked with people who had no sense of who God was. There was no awareness of godly guidance, almost no foundation in discerning values or morality, no understanding of what true love could be, and no sense of transcendence beyond the limitations of time or pain. They suffered because God was not real to them.

We who do have a relationship with God, however know the dark side of doing good. There is always too much to do. An overload of duty and need, dreams and would-be accomplishments distract us.

The call of the moment nags at us all day long. At such times we are not open to God's guidance. We can't hear the "holy whisper" in our hearts, because we are not listening. We have lost our sensitivity to the leading of the Spirit, so we cannot be led in a better way. We are disconnected from wisdom. It is not God who has caused the disconnection, but we who have failed to "log on," to keep open to our Source.

This same disconnect happens even when we are growing in God. Douglas John Hall writes that our temptation "is the desire to have arrived," "to transcend the precariousness of life," to be unwilling to *receive* God's life daily, "like the manna of the wilderness" or the "daily bread" of Jesus' model prayer."[10]

God's life is our daily bread and to intentionally make spaces in life to receive it is the only way to get what we perpetually ask for. Knowing the causes of suffering may be useful, but increasingly learning to trust will make a bigger difference. It has to do with allowing God entrance to our lives.

WHAT GOD CAN OR WILL DO

Is God an omnipotent, manipulative being who "makes" things happen? Or does God enter our lives, as Jesus and John so simply said, as "spirit" and as "love" (John 4:24, 1 John 4:16)? It is important to decide whether God forces or woos us, weakens or empowers us. We need to know whether God's power is used over us or for us, and whether that power is only outside us or can be in us.

As a child, I prayed that God would "make" things happen. I believed that God could do anything. But will God do anything? Surely God is not unlike good parents. They risk their children's safety and happiness countless times in order to let them become themselves, make their own decisions, and become wise and strong. They could "take over" in almost every case when a child is small. Parents have power, but loving parents don't always use it. Neither does God.

I think God is self-limited and have thought so since seminary days. Then some years ago I discovered that Thomas Aquinas thought so, too. He explained that God has absolute power, meaning that God can do anything. But Aquinas says that God has chosen to function in another manner, that God ordains or chooses to allow us some personal choice.[11] Thus we have a measure of freedom in which to respond to God and to exercise our own responsibility.

If we return to the analogy of parents and child, we cannot help but note that, compared to the child, the parents have enormous power. But for the child's sake, they do not use it all. Otherwise they would strip the child of freedom and initiative. The child would never discover its own weaknesses or strengths. It would never know the joy of learning, growth, or fulfillment, because it would be directed and shown everything it had to do. It could hardly be considered an individual. It would be merely an extension of its parents. It would probably never know gratitude or true love, for both are choices made with some measure of freedom.

So then, is everything that happens the will of God? If that is true, then God is the author of evil as well as good. If that is true, God wills wars and dead babies and drunk drivers. And if that is true, God wills that we sometimes disobey the commandments and ignore the words of Christ. That would mean that the God who commands us not to sin, makes us sin, and then, unbelievably, punishes us for it.

God acts in history. But how does God act? By manipulating people? By forcefully intervening? By changing natural law when necessary? Or does God act in history, not from the outside, but from the inside? Does God knock at the doors of human hearts to enter them and to win our wills, to influence us, the people who make history?

There are reasons for two creation stories in the Bible. Both are true in the deepest sense, but they are not the same. They need each other to give a whole picture. For one thing, God is imaged very differently by each of the two writers. First we are told of one whose being and power are far beyond our own, one whose domain encompasses the earth and goes far beyond all that we can see or know. This God, seemingly from the heavens, commands with a single word of power, and creation comes to be.

But God, as described by Genesis 2–3, stoops to the earth to give life. God digs in the ground, personally fashioning a human being from the inside out. Then, holding the body close, God breathes God's own spirit into that clay to give it life. It is this same God who walks and talks with Adam.

We need the God we have, a God with both aspects. We need a God who is almighty, who is wiser and greater than we. We pray to a God like that. And we need a God who touches us through our friends, who lives with us in our joys and sorrows, who speaks to us, within us, and even through us by the Holy Spirit.

In tragedy and suffering, it is important to know that God is greater than our need. But it may be even more important to welcome God into our space that may be filled with God's life.

Luther related this to the theology of the cross. God was poured out in Christ, sharing our pain, not reigning above us in almighty glory. Who among us does not cherish this God, a God who walks with us, leading us to green pastures, and also accompanies us through the valley of the shadow, restoring our souls? God was, is, and always will be that kind of God.

Elie Wiesel speaks of God like that. As a child, he was a survivor of Auschwitz. He tells of the hanging of a beautiful little Jewish boy in the concentration camp. It was a horrible death, watched in agony by those still surviving. The child took so long to die that a man from the back of the crowd began to cry out, "Where is God? Where is he?" Everyone waited, hardly able to bear each moment. Still the child did not die. The voice from behind cried out again, "Where is God now?" And within Wiesel someone answered, "Here he is—he is hanging here on this gallows."[12] Where is God when we suffer? With us in our pain. God is where we are.

RESPONDING TO SUFFERING

We can become bitter because of suffering. We can be exhausted and overcome. If suffering does not overwhelm us, we may be able to accept the grace to live with it and in spite of it. But some pain lasts for a lifetime. There are people who have never lived without it. In such cases no one knows its cause or has discovered a way to treat it in spite of extended searching.

Dorothee Soelle speaks of those who have come to the abandonment of hope and thus to clinical apathy. Suffering isolates people, she writes. They may come to a point where all they feel or see is their own suffering. It destroys the ability to communicate, and the sufferer becomes powerless and mute.

How then can healing come? Only by finding a voice, says Soelle. The imprisonment of pain must be destroyed. Sufferers must find a way to cry, to yell, to speak, to communicate, and to express their need. Religion must give people their voices. Once they can communicate, can objectively put feelings into words, they can begin to analyze their need. They can begin to organize with others in solidarity, to move from the language of emotion into rational expression, to decide what their objectives are, and, accepting where they are at the moment, to plan for conquest of their powerlessness through change, perhaps even radical change.[13]

GOD NEEDS US!

Earth has no meaning if it is a manipulated earth. Life has no worth if there is no choice, no risk, no consequence. Love is a choice, or it is worth nothing.

Hate and indifference are choices, too. God allows all of us to make them. Often, with or without thinking, we make choices that serve ourselves and not our neighbor. Those choices may even stunt or stop another life as, intent on our own personal goal, we forget how it will affect other people, their opportunities, their health, or their peace of mind. We live in a world with one another. Our choices affect our neighbors' lives.

Soelle writes about this compellingly in *Theology for Skeptics*. She addresses those who insist that "nothing happens without God's permission." And she speaks to those who believe that a God far above us and disconnected from us (sometimes called "the Wholly Other") has determined everything. She responds in terms of what Auschwitz taught sensitive German citizens:

> In reality everything depended on the lives and behavior of people in Germany for the victims of our actions. In reality everything relating to the preservation of this earth depends on the lives and behavior of people in the rich world. We are involved; we are responsible.
>
> In the Nazi period in Germany God was small and weak. God was in fact powerless because God had no friends. . . . God's spirit had no place to live. . . . The God who needs people in order to come into being was a nobody.[14]

It is the old profound understanding: we are the hands of God.

God does not run the world. God left that to us. But we cannot do it as God intends without the Holy Spirit and without faith. Yet the faith we need is more than a belief that God exists. We need a lived faith. We need to trust, to depend on the grace of God still pouring out since the first day of creation. Without it, God's will will not be done, nor will God's "kingdom come on earth as it is in heaven" where God is fully present.

God cannot stop injustice without finding people fearless enough to do it. God needs human ears to listen to the cries of peoples' pain. God needs human arms to hold those who need to be warmed by love. God, who gave us stewardship of our beloved earth, depends on us!

The church cannot be Christ's body and we cannot be its members unless it is Christ who lives within us and reaches out through us.

Suffering can "gift us" with strength. If we have not been weakened or destroyed, we become stronger. If we are no longer apathetic, we may actually discover serenity. Released and freed, at least in some measure, we can grow in compassion and gain far greater understanding for those whose need has some similarity to our own. God does not need to create pain to use it creatively.

We think of God sharing our suffering with us, but Luther makes us realize we can share God's enormous suffering. We can see and feel God's humanity, weakness, and foolishness in Christ; the humility and shame of the cross. In so doing, we can know God in ways we cannot experience through beauty, perfection, and glory. Through suffering for God and with God, we know God as we did not know before.

GOD IS WHERE WE ARE

We know God as the God of all creation and the God of eternity. We know God's love intimately as the rock on which we can always depend.

But that love is a gift, a grace that is offered. It has nothing to do with force, dominance, manipulation, power over others, or uninvolved authority. It has everything to do with sharing our life, our joys and challenges, and our suffering. It has everything to do with power offered for us and given to us. It has everything to do with us carrying on God's plan, with being God's people, and answering the eternal call.

Psalm 139 says that God is with us wherever we are, even when we dwell in darkness or among the dead! Wherever we may be, "Even there," cries the psalmist. "your hand shall lead me, and your right hand shall hold me fast" (Psalm 139:8-12).

God is where we are, wherever that is! God is with us even if we have so separated ourselves from God that we no longer know or feel it. Emmanuel is "God with us"! The Holy Spirit is God among us, within us, and reaching out from us.

God is where we are in our suffering and in our joy. God sees what we cannot see: the light within and beyond the darkness (Psalm 139:12). And sometimes we can see that light, too. We may be graced with joy, even in the midst of pain. We may be held in a "peace that passes understanding" in spite of anguish. Perhaps we will remember Paul rejoicing even while in prison (Philippians 4:4). Then we know that the light in the darkness is the enfolding presence of the great God who encompasses eternity. Then we realize that eternity includes here and now.

It is a perspective that we cannot afford to miss. So is the message of Christ preparing his followers for the days to come: "In the world you face persecution. But take courage; I have conquered the world!" (John 16:33).

THE HEART
GROWING IN GRACE

THE HOLY SPIRIT'S WORK OF LOVE

In the greater crises of my life, one set of sacred words has broken through the pain. My pastor father spoke them at my confirmation.

Thirteen of us knelt at the altar rail that Pentecost. I was thirteen. Nothing like this had ever happened to me before. Some part of me can still feel my father's hands upon my head. I can still hear the blessing repeated for each confirmand: thirteen times. I cherish the old words, composed to carry us through a lifetime, regardless of how difficult it might turn out to be:

> The Father in heaven, for Jesus' sake,
> renew and increase in you
> the gift of the Holy Spirit,
> to your strengthening in faith,
> to your growth in grace,
> to your patience in suffering,
> and to the blessed hope of everlasting life.[1]

"Amen," we answered, one by one. And in my heart there was something I could not then put into words: "Yes, God. I want that. I want your Spirit to live and grow in me!"

It took many years for me to put my head and heart together about that day. Was not the Holy Spirit given just once, at the birthday of the church, at Pentecost? How could the same gift be repeated? When the light broke for me, the whole Bible showed me the way. The Spirit, of course, is not a "thing" encapsulated within boundaries of space and time. The Spirit *is* life: dynamic, moving, vibrant life! It is the limitless energy that created the world and has always inspired and guided, comforted and healed. It was, is, and always will be available to us in inexhaustible supply.

Scripture tells us so. The very first words of the Bible are "In the beginning God created . . . And the Spirit of God moved upon the face of the waters." In the second creation story, God's life-giving Spirit is God's breath. Centuries later Job 33:4 testifies, "The breath of the Almighty keeps me alive." Still later, Jesus, in the synagogue at Capernaum, says simply, "It is the spirit that gives life" (John 6:63, NAB). The Nicene Creed has always proclaimed "the Spirit, the Lord, the giver of life. . . . [who] has spoken through the prophets." The Spirit was at work before Jesus ever came, before there was a church. It is the Spirit who was here before all things, gave life to all, and ever calls us to itself.

Jesus put it together ever so simply. In three words he defined God to the woman at the well, saying, "God is spirit" (John 4:24). Then Paul, in 2 Corinthians 3:17 wrote, "The Lord is Spirit."

In *The Spiritual Life*, Evelyn Underhill writes that God is like the atmosphere, surrounding everything on earth.[2] If that is so (and the doctrine of omnipresence sounds very much like that), we are immersed in God. We constantly breathe in the air without thinking. In faith we can consciously drink in God's Spirit. The God who fills heaven and earth and all that is fills us as well. Ephesians 3:19 calls it being "filled with the fullness of God."

Surely that is what Frances Ridley Havergal realized when she wrote in her hymn "Lord, Speak to Me":

> O fill me with thy fullness, Lord,
> until my very heart o'erflow
> In kindling thought and glowing word,
> thy love to tell, thy praise to show.[3]

It is the Spirit that filled Jesus and overflowed his heart and life. It is the same Spirit that Jesus gives to those who receive him, follow him, and believe in him. It is the Spirit that sanctifies: makes us more than we have been and empowers us to know and share God's truth, love, and power.

Luther called the Spirit "the Sanctifier" and wrote, "God . . . created us for this very purpose, to redeem and sanctify us."[4] If that is true, anyone can "grow in grace." It is possible because we are immersed in the presence of our ever-faithful, ever-gracious God.

Growing in grace leads to grace growing in us. We pray earnestly for it, crying, "Come, Holy Spirit!" God cannot say no to such a plea, for it was God who formed it in our hearts.

Even Christ grew—"grew in grace and truth." And he is our pattern. We can grow that way as well. That is our calling: to grow in God and toward God and to share it with others. It is also our need. We cannot handle the increasing burdens of life unless we are also growing in our relationship to the one whose strength is all we have.

SANCTIFICATION AND BAPTISM

Sanctification is the term used for such growth in grace. It is a word that has not always been understood. Literally it means "to make holy," that is, to be drawn closer and closer to the one who is holy. It means that God's will can increasingly become our own and we can live it.

Sanctification does not mean we strive for perfection or attain it on earth, although many have so counseled. Luther, too, in 1516 preached on sanctification as stages of beginning, progressing, and then coming to perfection. But later he often made it clear that such perfection does not occur until after death. His *Large Catechism* states, "The Holy Spirit carries on his work unceasingly until the last day."[5]

Sanctification also does not mean that we imitate Christ in some external ways. On that subject, Luther urged his followers to "conform" to Christ instead, to have such a relationship to Christ that we would grow to become more like him. In such a case, sanctification would be a natural result, not a spiritually self-centered goal. It would also be interior, not dependent on external actions. God claims our hearts, and from inside-out, we respond with "Yes!" The external results of faith (works) follow.[6]

Some speak of sanctification as though we can work at it, hoping to achieve it "without the grace of the Holy Spirit." *The Formula of Concord* defines this as Pelagianism.[7] But sanctification is actually God's work in us, God's transformation of our spirits, our loves, our goals, our lives. Our part is to receive and to believe: to open our hearts in trust and then to live in trust, committed to God and to God's world. That is faith, a living thing that must be constantly renewed and supported by the Spirit. It begins, says the church, at baptism. In that ceremony, says Lutheran Bishop H. George Anderson, "we are empowered for a life of daily transformation." He describes Luther's point of view refreshingly:

> Baptism is not a ten-minute ceremony that happens to babies. It takes a lifetime to complete. Martin Luther called baptism 'the daily garment which the Christian is to wear all the time.' That is, the pattern of our Christian life comes from the continuous arc of baptism—being brought low, washed, and then raised up. Every day is a new experience of that cycle: recognizing our sin, remembering that we are baptized as children of God, and then being invigorated by the assurance of forgiveness.[8]

For me the phrase "I am baptized" means that God is always giving life. I am always making mistakes, always becoming estranged from others, thinking or wanting or doing things that are not what I want to think or want or do. I need to ask to be forgiven, to be empowered to begin again, over and over. And God claims me, accepts me just as I am, receives my repentance, forgives me, encourages me to start over, and offers me new life. I let go of who I was and begin again to become a new person. It is like dying and rising in God all the time.

There is a practical side to this. Bishop Anderson speaks of daily self-examination with Christ's life as our measure and inspiration. There are questions we need to ask ourselves, he says: "What in my past is prohibiting me from doing what I need to do today?" "Who can't I talk to because I'm nursing a grudge?" "What am I limited from doing by unresolved conflicts?" Questions like these make the theory and theology of baptism real.

Bishop Anderson also comments on how baptism frees him to "sin boldly" in his daily life. He is, of course, speaking of Luther's counsel to be willing to take risks, to be willing to be wrong, for otherwise we are too insecure to accomplish anything for God. He admits, as must we all, that sometimes God's guidance is not clear to us, even though we know God is where we are. The bishop's words here are worth remembering: "In that kind of situation baptism allows me to realize God is present in the decision, more like a coach helping me get through the race than a judge who's going to determine whether I came in first, second, or last."[9]

FAITH AS CONTINUAL RECEPTIVITY

In *The Preface to the Romans*, Luther insists that since sin and old desires still linger in faith-filled people, "both the gifts and the Spirit must be received by us daily."[10]

Luther writes in *Two Kinds of Righteousness* that "by grace alone the Father inwardly draws us to Christ," gifting us with a righteousness that is not our own. It is "instilled" in us, he says, "not all at once, but . . . begins, makes progress, and is finally perfected at the end through death."[11] Our earthy selves are touched by the fire of God, and gradually, yielding, we are sanctified. Luther wrote, "Just as the heated iron glows like fire because of the union of fire with it, so the Word imparts its qualities to the soul."[12] We are the iron, warmed by the glowing, outpouring fire of God and united to the fire by its self-giving love.

In one of his Weimar sermons, Luther said:

> Since Christ comes into our heart through the gospel, he must also be accepted by the heart. As I now believe that he is in the gospel, so I receive him and have him already. So Paul says: "I carry Christ in my heart, for he is mine." (Ephesians 3:17)[13]

Paul speaks of this transformative change in several places. In 2 Corinthians 5:17, he states, "So if anyone is in Christ, there is a new creation: everything old has passed away; see, everything has become new!" That includes us! We become "new creatures." Paul underscores this with his powerful statement in Galatians 2:20: "It is no longer I who live, but it is Christ who lives in me."

Luther understands well what Paul is saying. He explains that the "I" who no longer lives is "a person distinct from God," a person who seeks complete autonomy. We might explain this as a self-sufficient person, such as one who believes themselves master of his or her own soul, responsible to no one else and caring about no one else. Such a person feels no need for God and ignores the constant influence of the Spirit. It is such an "I" that God yearns to replace in order that a new attachment may be formed. Luther explains: "Christ is fixed and cemented to me and abides in me. The life I now live, he lives in me. . . . Christ and I are one. . . . This attachment to Him causes me to be . . . pulled out of my own skin, and transferred into Christ and into His kingdom, which is a kingdom of grace, righteousness, peace, joy, life, salvation, and eternal glory."[14] This gift of grace is the fulfilling of the process described in chapter 6, where we discussed the movement from self to Self.

We have noted that Luther frequently affirmed that God's work in us is not completed until our earthly life is over. He states that poignantly in the following words:

This life, therefore, is not righteousness,
but growth in righteousness;
not health, but healing;
not being, but becoming;
not rest, but exercise.
We are not yet what we shall be,
but we are growing toward it.
The process is not yet finished,
but it is going on.
This is not the end,
but it is the road.
All does not yet gleam in glory,
but all is being purified.[15]

St. Paul had a way of saying something quite similar: "And all of us, with unveiled faces, seeing the glory of the Lord as though reflected in a mirror, are transformed into the same image from one degree of glory to another; for this comes from the Lord, the Spirit" (2 Corinthians 3:18).

People *do* grow in grace. We have all seen it. They may have become more selfless, more gentle, more generous, more forgiving. Some become more willing to be helped or stronger in the face of temptation and pain. Some learn the grace of waiting, living more patiently with mysteries and struggles they cannot quite understand. Some discover that learning to love is life's greatest fulfillment, not money or "success," position or power. And many let go of thinking they must be perfect.

When I see this in others I know I can stop trying so hard to make life and myself what I believe they ought to be. At those times I can hear Christ's gentle words, "Don't be anxious. See the lilies of the field." "Don't be afraid. You believe in God; believe also in me."

It is the gift of the Spirit that initiates and empowers our growth in grace. It is that gift that our heavenly parent offers to give, not just once, but to renew and to increase. That is why my confirmation blessing continues to lift me up.

I cannot see what light or darkness is before me, but I will hold fast in my heart to those precious words that I know I will take to my death:

The Father in heaven, for Jesus' sake,
renew and increase in you
the gift of the Holy Spirit,

to your strengthening in faith,
to your growth in grace,
to your patience in suffering,
and to the blessed hope of everlasting life.

REFORMATION:
GROWING SPIRITUALLY AS A CHURCH

Most of the time when we speak of "church growth," we refer to growth in the numbers of people the church can claim as members. Yet the truer growth of the church is not a matter of statistics but of the Spirit working in and through the body of Christ. It is not a matter of accumulating people but of speaking to people's true needs, whether they are inside or outside the organization.

Of course, growth in grace is not just a matter for individuals. It is deeply important in the organization and functioning of the church itself. We are in grave danger whenever the church sees itself beyond reform or change, as spiritually pure or whole. Luther obviously recognized that, for he insisted that "the church must always be reformed."[16] True reformation, of course, is not primarily a matter of exteriors. It begins on the inside through inspired people and reforming movements throughout history. The church has been called to something deeper than what can be seen. It has been called to sanctification, to growth in wisdom and love. Without this, its effectiveness could not have been sustained. True life is impossible without periodic purification, adaptation, and change.

The church cannot live without continuing reformation. Luther's call to "die daily" is strong medicine and something of a shock when one thinks of it in terms of the organization of the body of Christ. The daily dying that Luther called for means to let go of anything that fractures our common ministry. It means to let go of whatever stands in the way of empowering, transformative love. It means to let self-centeredness die, to let go of anything that stands between God and our relationships with each other.

This is what continual reformation is: the process of purification, of stretching exercises, of the grace of growth, and of healing. Begun and continued by grace, it includes repentance and forgiveness; discipleship and discipline; letting go and adding on; commitment to God and cooperation with each other.

We are all called. We are called to continual transformation of ourselves, our church, and the world. But we cannot do it! Only God can do it. And God will do it in us and through us, if we say yes.

Reformation, Repentance, and Empowerment

Reformation and repentance are interlocked. It is no accident that Luther's *Ninety-five Theses* begins with the subject of repentance. Without it, no reformation could ever happen. Luther wrote, "When our Lord and Master Jesus Christ said, 'Repent' (Matthew 4:17), he willed the entire life of believers to be one of repentance." Thus, continuing reformation is empowered by continuing repentance until the end of life.[17]

So often we think of repentance as being stuck in the grime of guilt rather than being freed to new possibilities; as self-punishment rather than heartfelt reception of God's forgiving grace.

Luther asked for both inner and outer repentance, a purging of our insidious self-centeredness as well as a new way of life, a "re-forming" of life. Luther knew that resurrection is always connected with some kind of death.

Repentance is a word for radical change, for turning in a new direction. It begins with honesty and ends in freedom. *Repentance* is a word of sorrow and a word of hope.

Reformation should not mean just "breaking away from" something or from each other. It is a letting go of old attitudes, habits, understandings, and ways that do not give life. Its greater purpose is increased wholeness and unity in the Spirit, a better comprehension of God's way in our own time, and a movement toward the fulfilling of that will.

But repentance is not our only need. Something else stands in the way of true reformation. It is the fear to stick our necks out. In Old Testament terms, it is the fear of being prophetic. Laity and clergy alike are infected with this fear. The church of the Reformation teaches the "ministry of all believers," but most of us need to learn to believe it and dare to live it.

That is possible only through the promise and the gift of the Holy Spirit. We can hardly believe that God really does enter and empower people like us! Yet the church exists only because God poured out the Spirit on *all* people who would receive it, who "heard the word" with their hearts (Acts 10:44).

Even the most ordinary member of the church has an extraordinary calling. Each and every one of us is asked to be a light in the darkness, a voice in the emptiness, a hand reaching into loneliness. Each of us is needed to share our joy and to add our strength as part of the healing of the world and creation from wherever we stand within it.

Every one of us is needed! But the church could die unless a true ministry of the laity becomes a reality very soon. We need a new reformation, a reformation in which the laity are empowered!

The Spirit of life is a spirit of fire, a wind, a breath of fresh air. The Spirit *moves* continually. And if it moves, neither we nor the church can be a frozen structure, glued to some small part of the past and closed to all ideas but our own.

The Spirit is not the possession of a few people in particular positions. It does not come to us by training of the brain but by the opening of the heart and yielding of the will. Jesus had no position in society or the religious hierarchy. Yet the Spirit lived and breathed through him who prayed, "Thy will, not mine, be done."

Perhaps we are called to "bloom where we are planted." Or maybe we are asked to make a radical change in attitude, location, training, or lifestyle. Surely we are not called to be great or to do great things in order to boost our ego. Life is precious even if it is not spectacular, and each of us is called to bless the world, to give it life, and to empower it.

A magnificent promise is given us: "You will receive power when the Holy Spirit has come upon you; and you will be my witnesses . . . to the ends of the earth" (Acts 1:8).

THE LIFE-GIVING HEART

GOD'S LIFE THROUGH US

The one who believes in me . . . will do greater works than these, because I am going to my Father.

—John 14:12

The fourteenth through sixteenth chapters of the Gospel of John were, for Luther, some of his favorite scripture, and they are mine.

Reading them is like entering the room where the Last Supper is being held. Except for Jesus, Judas, you, and me, no one there realizes that this is the final time together.

Jesus is speaking tenderly, but his words are frightening to his friends. He knows how much needs to be said at this celebration. Yet in spite of all he says, one quiet but shocking message is all the disciples seem to hear. He simply says, "I must go away."

For a moment we step back from our own involvement, step back to look at the story as it has been told by John. We imagine details that John omitted: feelings, statements, and tone of voice.

∾

"How can you leave us, Jesus? We have left everything for you: jobs and homes and families! Our people have waited for centuries for the Messiah! We thought you were the one!

"In some ways you are more than we hoped for. You are more than our master. You have looked into our eyes and called us 'friends.' You have given us reason to live!

"You have shown us what it means to let go of anything that stands in the way of love. You have empowered us to heal. When we thought we were weak, you made us strong.

"No, Jesus. You can't go. We can't bear it! What would we do?"

The words of their teacher seem earthshaking to his friends.

Again they insist: "No, Jesus! No one can take your place. Never has anyone spoken like you. Never has anyone lived or loved or taught like you. Never has anyone brought such life into our confused and weary world!"

Then Jesus looks at them and says: "The one who believes in me . . . will do greater works than these, because I go to the Father."

"Greater? How is that possible? Because you are going away? What can you mean?"

And he answers: "I will send you one who will stand beside you and live within you. All the days of your life he will be your comforter. Those who have not known me will not understand. But you will understand naturally because you already are acquainted with the one whom I will send. He has been with you all this time, living in me. He has spoken through me and healed through me. He has loved people to life through my eyes and in my touch. When I have gone, you will not be able to depend upon me as you have before. But he will still be here. Then you will know he lives in you.

"Unless I go, you will not know his presence or his power. You will always depend upon me beside you. But now it is time for you to realize that *the Spirit who lives in me is sent to live in you.*

"Claim the Spirit! The Spirit says, 'I am yours!' You must respond, 'And I am yours!' Then offer up your prayer: '*O Spirit of my Lord, the Christ, be the fire within my heart, the thought within my brain, and the words upon my lips! Speak to me and through me! Reach out from me and do your work! Be the life of my life so that all I do is what you do through me*'" (author's paraphrase and addition).

◡

I deeply believe that to receive God's life and then to give it away is the reason God put us all on earth. If that is true, it is the most thrilling of all reasons to be alive! What can be more exciting than to awaken people to their dignity, their potential, and their sacred identity, the person whom God sees in them? What can be better than helping others discover they are strong enough to be givers too? What can be more wonderful than to draw forth from human beings their creative passion, to open doors for them and offer them support, to help them learn how to fill a need and consequently to find a task that is their own? We are called to empowerment. We are called to give life.

Without exception, every mother I know tells me that giving birth was the most awesome experience of her life. But we do not need to bear children to fulfill that call. If we have the eyes to see and heart to recognize it, we can give life every day of our lives, in every direction we turn.

Our lives are our ministries. Even though we cannot give ourselves life, we can give it to each other! And except through occupations that are degrading or greedy, we can give life almost anywhere, in countless ways.

But we cannot give without receiving. We are barren without grace. There is no way to be a channel of God's life without drinking it in, without allowing God to touch and fill us, without opening our hearts to receive the perfect, healing love of the Holy Spirit. That is what living receptively is all about.

We are given the Spirit in order to love God back and to touch other lives with the Spirit's fire. We are each a spark given life because we matter to God. But we have also been ignited by that fire to set other lives ablaze with the same life-giving power.

SALVATION: FORGIVENESS, HEALING, WHOLENESS, AND LIBERATION

Do you remember your dreams of growing up? Did anyone ever help you to understand that by God's grace you could make a difference in other people's lives?

My parents did. Probably because of their influence, the words of a poem picked up in college burned into my brain. I have never forgotten them.

> Speak to us, Lord, until our hearts are melted
> to share in thy compassion for the lost.
> 'Til our souls yearn, with burning intercession,
> that they may know thy name, whate'er the cost.[1]

For me those words meant "God, show me how to help others know that you exist. Give me a way to help them know how much you love them. Touch them through me, even if I do not know it, so that they will welcome your wonderful Spirit to live in them and love others to life as well."

We worship a God who began all existence by loving us to life. That life giving has never stopped. We follow and call ourselves by the name of one who said he came to give abundant life, who said, "I am the resurrection and the life. Those who believe in me, even though they die, will live, and everyone who lives and believes in me will never die" (John 11:25-26). The earth that God created has, in countless ways, been recreated through the life of Christ. And that life, through the energy of the Holy Spirit, has continued to re-create through dedicated people again and again. It is clear that God intends to keep on giving life, giving through anyone who is willing to be led by the power of the Spirit.

Luther wrote in "The Freedom of a Christian":

> Why should I not . . . joyfully, with all my heart and with an eager will, do all things which . . . are pleasing . . . to such a Father who has overwhelmed me with his inestimable riches? I will therefore give myself as a Christ to my neighbor, just as Christ offered himself to me.[2]

Writing in the same vein about John 14:20, Luther explained:

> This is the first main point by which man soars out of himself and beyond himself into Christ. Then there is a descent from above. Just as I am in Christ, so Christ, in turn, is in me. . . . Now he also manifests himself in me and says: "Go forth, preach, comfort, baptize, serve your neighbor, be obedient, be patient. I will be in you and will do all this. Whatever you do will be done by me. Just be of good cheer, be bold, and trust in me. See that you remain in me; then I, in turn, will surely be in you."[3]

Salvation is not only what Christ offered us through his life, death, and resurrection. Nor is it just eternal life in heaven. It is what God's life is doing in us right now! It is the whole process of reconciliation and sanctification. Paul says in 1 Corinthians 1:18 that we "are being saved."

To understand salvation in this way is to see it as the healing of our own brokenness and of broken relationships. It is the breaking down of walls that divide us from God, from others, and from ourselves. It is the beginning of the coming of the kingdom even as we look for a day when that will be perfectly fulfilled.

Too often those who have nothing in this world have been taught to put all hope in a heaven hereafter. But Jesus spoke far more about God's kingdom on earth than about God's kingdom in heaven.[4] His theme song certainly was not "Soon I will be done with the troubles of the world. . . . Goin' away to live with God." His ministry was one of justice, of healing, and liberation. His point was that *God is here, in every now that ever is, in time*!

The contemporary Catholic theologian, Rosemary Radford Ruether, argues a similar point:

> Only when redemption [salvation] . . . is understood as histor-
> ical, as . . . God's original intention for creation, rather than a
> rejection of creation, will it become possible to see . . . equality
> in Christ as a mandate, not merely of flight from the world,
> but of transformation of the world in . . . justice.[5]

Even the church has been guilty of sanctioning an oppressive status quo for the sake of peace and order. That was its usual approach in Latin America, from the time of the Spanish conquest until recently. That desire for peace at the price of growth and freedom is what has kept the church from acknowledging the power of the Holy Spirit in the lives of ordinary people, for, of course, a spiritual revolution could become economic, social, and political as well.

Fortunately there are those who have heard Jesus proclaim his mission in the words of Isaiah 61 (also Luke 4) and have made it their own. Jesus came to give hope for despair; to give sight to sightless eyes and muddled minds; to liberate us from habits, compulsions, people, and situations that imprison us; to offer life-giving forgiveness and teach us to forgive. In the Isaiah version that Jesus read, the proclamation goes even further:

> The Spirit of the Lord . . . has anointed me . . .
> to comfort all who mourn . . .
> to give them a garland instead of ashes,
> the oil of gladness instead of mourning,
> the mantle of praise instead of a faint spirit;
> They will be called oaks of righteousness,
> the planting of the Lord, to display his glory. (1-3)

This is the message of a life giver! "To give them a garland instead of ashes" is to give life where death is near at hand. It is to plant hope where there is disillusionment, apathy, ignorance, and powerlessness. It is to personally hang on and to lift up others when everyone else is letting go and pulling down their families or associates or friends.

Every year my youngest undergraduate students seem more hopeless about the world than those of the year before. They ask, "Dr. Brame, why shouldn't I just give up? I am only one. What can anyone do in the face of so much evil and greed? How do you handle it?"

I have to answer: "It's hard! I have many days when I see no way out, when there is no energy to fight, and almost no will to hope. But I know that I can choose to be part of the problem or the solution. Sometimes I remember the Chinese proverb associated with the Christophers: 'It is better to light one candle than to curse the darkness.'"

Dorothy Day once wrote:

> Young people say what good can one person do? What is the sense of our small effort? They cannot see that we must lay one brick at a time, take one step at a time. We can be responsible only for the one action of the present moment. But we can beg for an increase of love in our hearts that will vitalize and transform all our individual actions and know that God will take them and multiply them, as Jesus multiplied the loaves and fishes.[6]

"My life is all I have to give," I tell them. "I desperately want it to count for something I believe in. I want it to be part of God's creative work. I want to give life, even if it is to only one person!"

We need to have eyes to see both the goodness and evil, beauty and ugliness, hopelessness and hope that are a part of our world. All are real. And all must be dealt with. Without a balanced perspective, we are naive and cannot be discriminating or responsible. Without the ability to evaluate, we may give ourselves up to the prevailing wind or "call evil good and good evil."

I give almost all of my students a means of discernment gained from Paul Tillich: that whatever is creative is godly and that which is destructive (of the good) is demonic. If we can discern between the creative and destructive, we can find direction, meaning, and hope.

We are left with the choice to give up or to go on, to use even the last bit of life for something that will matter, or to let life "do us in."

In her inimitable manner, Evelyn Underhill writes in *The Ways of the Spirit*:

> Redemption is not just you and me made safe and popped into heaven. It means that each soul, redeemed from self-interest by

the revelation of Divine Love, is taken and used again for the spread of that redeeming work.[7]

Even the least of us is commissioned by Christ: "I chose you. And I appointed you to go and bear fruit, fruit that will last" (John 15:16). Luther responds, saying that true faith will bear fruit, for "[f]aith without works is like fire without heat or light."[8]

It is God's Spirit within us that does the work, as John 14:17 has made clear: "The Spirit abides [not only] with you, [but] he will be in you." So Luther writes, "Our works are then good, when he alone is wholly their agent in us."[9] Eckhart had commented in his sermons:

> Above all, claim nothing for yourself. Relax and let God oper-ate in you and do what he will with you. The deed is his; the word is his; this birth is his; and all you are is his, for you have surrendered self to him, with all your soul's agents and their functions and even your personal nature.[10]

God wants to do your work himself.[11]

NOTICING PEOPLE

Giving life to others begins by noticing them. Remember how Jesus noticed the "invisible people"? There was Zacchaeus, short and looked down upon, who had to climb a tree to see Jesus. Jesus noticed and invited himself to dinner at Zacchaeus' house. There was the woman at the well, a scorned Samaritan, of whom Jesus asked a cup of water under the scorching sun. To her amazement, he told her who she really was and offered her another water, eternally life-giv-ing. There was the woman who washed his feet with her tears and perfumed his hair and took up his time. He gave it happily. There was a woman being stoned to death until he stopped it and chal-lenged those who accused her. There were the "untouchables," whom he touched in love and healed.

No one can be an instrument of deep healing without noticing and affirming the presence and worth of another. Concern, love, and caring give life. Indifference is worse than hatred. It kills in a silent, subtle, draining way. *The ignored will not cry out, "Please notice me!"* Indifference leaves them powerless.

We need to remember the strength given by acknowledgment, the meeting of eyes, the recognition by name, the awareness of a unique gift, the affirmation of a job well done, the support of others doing their best. These are signs of grace, God's giving.

A name says, "Here I am!" It identifies a particular self, a self that counts and has worth. God understands the power of calling a person by name. Isaiah 43:1 says, "Do not fear, for I have redeemed you; I have called you by name, you are mine." By speaking our name, God gives us identity.

Martin Buber's tiny but important work on identity made an impression on the twentieth century. _I and Thou_ pointed out to all of us that we may choose to treat another person as an object, as a thing, as an "it."[12] But we can also recognize another with respect; we can acknowledge the other with awe, as a "thou." We can recognize God as "the Ultimate Thou" above all others. Buber's work made such an impression on one of my students that she put a sign on her dormitory door in large letters: "I AM A THOU!" For her it was a declaration, an emancipation from a situation that she could not previously name.

If anyone knew the power of "noticing" people, Mother Teresa did. She said, "The biggest disease today is not leprosy or tuberculosis, but rather the feeling of being unwanted, uncared-for, and deserted by everybody. _The greatest evil is . . . the terrible indifference towards one's neighbor._"[13]

I remember hearing someone tell of Mother Teresa's first days in Calcutta. She had gone out on the street to search out "the poorest of the poor" for whom she intended to live the rest of her life. She saw an old, sick body in a gutter. Going closer she realized that she had come upon a man who was dying. His emaciated body was covered with sores oozing pus. Maggots were on his skin. She bent down, clasped the body to her in all its disgusting filth, and began to minister to him. Someone later asked, "How _could_ you?" and her reply was, simply, "I saw Jesus."

That was always her way of looking at others. She looked for Jesus in every face. She ministered to Jesus. Matthew 25:35-36, 40 was real to her:

> I was hungry and you gave me food, I was thirsty and you gave me something to drink. I was a stranger and you welcomed me, I was naked and you gave me clothing, I was sick and you took care of me, I was in prison and you visited me. . . . Just as you did it to one of the least of these . . . , you did it to me.

Malcolm Muggeridge wrote in *Something Beautiful for God* that Mother Teresa's intention was "to hear in the cry of every abandoned child, even in the tiny squeak of the discarded fetus, the cry of the Bethlehem child; to recognize in every leper's stumps the hands which once touched sightless eyes and made them see."[14]

Mother Teresa once wrote:

> O beloved sick, how doubly dear you are to me, when you personify Christ; and what a privilege is mine to be allowed to tend you. . . . And O God, while you are Jesus, my patient, deign also to be to me a patient Jesus, bearing with my faults, looking only to my intention, which is to love and serve you in the person of each of your sick.[15]

She was sensitive to something most of us are still learning: there is an unseen holiness in every human being. Each is born to be an expression of God's life. And you and I are here to help each other recognize that transforming truth in ourselves and in each other. We can only begin by seeing the intrinsic value of every living thing on earth.

That value is not based on how people or the rest of creation can be used for someone else's gain. Intrinsic value is the value each has in the eyes of God who treasures them, and it is the value they have to themselves. What more than life matters to each of us, except to love and be loved?

It is for this reason that we must become aware of those "who are set off, shut out, locked up or chained down":[16] the children chained to machines in sweatshops who make our clothes; their young mothers, locked into factories daily, given one insufficient meal a day, rarely allowed to go to the bathroom, working for starvation wages so that conglomerates can have greater sales and pay stockholders larger dividends. Most of us have no idea how much of an ordinary consumer's comfort depends on the sacrifice and suffering of the nameless and unseen here and beyond our borders. We do not realize that if they were paid just a bit more, they might not die early. If we were really aware of all the facts, we would rebel! How could anyone know of such pain and do nothing to change the way we function?[17]

Yet, as a friend of mine sighs, "I have compassion fatigue. There is too much to do and too many who need help!" What caring person has not felt that way, perhaps for years? But Thomas Kelly, a Quaker, steps in with counsel, saying, "We cannot die on every cross, nor are we expected to."[18]

We live in a world of limitation. We have only one life to give, and we want to use it wisely and well. Even Christ could be only at one place at one time. He had ears and eyes and arms to listen, see, and touch only one person or one group at a time. Once, we read, he withdrew from a sick, needy crowd that pleaded for his attention, in order to draw apart for the refreshment of prayer. We know he prayed often. He slept, he ate, and he took time to notice the lilies of the field, resting in the care of God. We cannot expect to do more than Jesus.

What did he tell us and show us about dealing with the need of others? He seemed to move back and forth from the needs of the crowds to the needs of the person. Were he on earth today, he would surely pay attention to individuals as well as to community, national, and global needs. But again, not all at once. Elton Trueblood speaks about "living in chapters," that is, living one phase at a time, putting most of our energies into one mission and trying to do that well.

Marjorie Thompson writes in the spirituality journal *Weavings*:

> It will be important to select just one or two things that you can do realistically and well. . . . The one who is faithful in small things has more impact than the one who is unfaithful in large endeavors. But whatever you do, *choose something* (emphasis added)![19]

Many caring people choose a mission that is face-to-face, that is personal. They choose one person, one family, or one group to bless in whatever way they can. They are "there for them." They "adopt" a person to provide what is needed most: friendship, clothing, help with studies, an introduction to a larger world, perhaps financial support, counseling, encouragement, a listening ear, or even a home. There are people who change the lives of one person at a time by being a "big brother" or serving (and listening) at church-supported meals. Some work to provide food or clothing, or they tutor children or adults in the inner city. And there are many painting and hammering, fixing up old houses or building for Habitat for Humanity.

God has given a second chance to many of us who might well have lost our lives. We sometimes wonder why we are still on earth. Perhaps it is to make the life of one who feels insignificant more hopeful and more full.

But none of us can afford to completely forget the larger picture, the faceless, nameless millions of the poor whose labor sustains the comfortable and the better off. Hebrew scripture call them the *anawim*. Their plight is one of our greatest tragedies.

Some individuals who have the funds are making "alternative investments." That means they will take risks on low-return loans to help people buy their own farms or businesses. Some invest only in companies that reflect their values: businesses that do not employ children, that pay laborers a living wage, that do not lock in their employees or work them without rest, that feed them healthy, sufficient meals. Guiding these efforts is the Interfaith Council on Corporate Responsibility (ICCR), affiliated with the National Council of Churches. At the same time, the National Labor Committee is struggling for the rights of workers in sweatshops across the world.[20]

With the coming of the year 2000, a groundbreaking project was begun. Jubilee 2000 is working to enable large monetary gifts to reach their designated destination rather than go to dictators or Mafia. Churches around the world are challenging governments to reduce or cancel monies owed by debtor nations who can never recover without such aid. This effort will continue in some form, it is hoped, for decades to come.[21]

I look for the day when our media will pay attention to far more than the United States and Europe. I hope for the time when it will focus on some of those who have never been seen, those whom Hebrew scripture calls the *anawim*, the powerless and the poor. God waits to draw us all to a time of hope and healing.

LIBERATION SPIRITUALITY

With the ending of Vatican II in 1965, the Catholic Church was sensitized to a more helpful and healthy way to help the poor than through charity, simply giving money and goods to those in need. The church called for adding a program of education and empowerment of the disenfranchised.

Then in 1968, the Latin American Episcopal Conference (CELAM) of the Catholic Church held a groundbreaking meeting in Medellin, Colombia. It asked: "Who are the people of God?" It recognized that the primary characteristic of the people of Asia, Africa, and South America was poverty. From that meeting came a historic declaration, "a preferential option for the poor" whom Christ so passionately loved. Another CELAM meeting in 1979 reaffirmed this position, and the World Council of Churches followed with its support, as well.

Unfortunately these actions were viewed as a threat by some powerful governments and industries. To speak for the poor, outstanding "liberation theologians" such as Gustavo Gutiérrez, Jon Sobrino, and Leonardo and Clodovis Boff arose in South and Central America. Many compassionate bishops and missionaries put their lives on the line. Some were martyred. Rome attempted to silence several individuals whom it deemed dangerous or believed to be Marxist.

But "liberation theology" would not be silenced. Strong voices wrote about the ideals of helping people establish "base communities" of cooperative support, Bible study, and assertive action techniques with employers. It was not a fad. It was an approach that will always be needed wherever people are powerless and poor.

I personally use the term "liberation spirituality," meaning a dynamic, living spiritual relationship with God and others that frees people to be all that God intends. It is an assertive but pacifist claim to power that engenders respect for all parties involved and denigrates or enfeebles no one. I strongly believe that our inherent human power is given to be used *for* each other and not *over* each other. Obviously such a spirituality is cooperative and not hierarchical.

Obviously it is also biblical. Christ's proclamation of "bringing good news" and "freeing those who are imprisoned" undergirds this approach. So do the words of the Beatitudes and the preaching of prophets such as Amos. This practical approach is now influencing movements among the poor in the United States, particularly among blacks and those of Latin heritage. Its leaders and participants are Protestant and Catholic alike.

Let me point to the work of a young woman, Mev Puleo, whose work has inspired both me and my students. In 1996 she died of brain cancer at the age of thirty, but her life had already been influential.

She was fourteen years old when she took a Brazilian tour bus up a mountain to see the majestic statue of Christ the Redeemer with hands outstretched over the city of Rio de Janeiro. It was then that she experienced her first real awareness of the difference between the lives of rich and poor. Looking out the windows of the bus, she saw,

on one side, large, luxurious apartment buildings set in parklike settings. On the other side of the road, she saw pitiable shacks, squalor,
dirt, and pain. One side seemed to have everything; the other side,
nothing. Above it all stood the Christ!

Vowing to do something about it, she worked to become an
excellent photographer and interviewer, and before she died, she
authored and illustrated her book, *The Struggle Is One*. There she
placed the thoughts of nineteen Brazilian leaders in liberation spirituality: women and men, Catholic and Protestant, people of prestige
and simple people who incarnate greatness.[22]

I often use Puleo's book at the end of a graduate course in contemporary spirituality. In every case it has moved the mature students
deeply, sometimes causing some life-changing decisions. The book's
greatest gift to both my students and myself has been the courage of
the women Puleo interviewed. We read of those who give up marriage because of *machismo* (which we would term "macho") attitudes
but take on whole families to support and nurture. These are women
who have helped to form the "base communities" spoken of above.
Through them, people discover their rights, learn how to organize,
develop skills, and gain employment. Together they work for fair
working conditions and better wages.

Regular Bible study is the most basic and most important function of the base communities. Scriptures are studied by each person
who asks what the message means for them. Then they are personally
and corporately applied.

But the effort does not end there. The members of base communities take solidarity seriously. They try to help each other to recognize
their individual identity in God and to realize the power of the Holy
Spirit within each of them. They call the process *conscientization*, the
forming of a critical consciousness regarding the social and cultural situation while awakening to their own capacity to transform it.[23]
Together they work to educate and empower each other to be leaders
who can pull people together and effectively negotiate with employers.
Some of them have gone a step further by attaining cooperative ownership of their companies.[24]

Base communities are an example for all of us to learn how to
encourage and support those who have nothing. Participation in such
communities is prophetic living. One must be willing to work for

change, regardless of the cost. The approach of these communities to the Bible, to cooperative effort, to conscious confrontation of their need, and to living out love of God and neighbor has in it the simplest and truest strain of Christianity. Would that we could learn from them!

PASSION

Matthew Fox writes in *Original Blessing*, "To settle for a heart that is indifferent to others is to refuse to imitate the Creator." He says, "In the Bible it is coldness of heart, not hate, that is the opposite of love. This is why Dante makes ice and not fire represent the lowest pit of hell." It is not caring, losing our passion, that robs us of compassion and leads us into sin.[25]

Eckhart's belief that "all deeds are accomplished in passion" says that if we care we have power. Passion is the power that is indispensable when we come to facing the almost impossible tasks of feeding, clothing, housing, educating, and *empowering* a world full of the forgotten and oppressed.[26]

Joan Chittister, a Benedictine nun and writer, writes in her monthly reflections, *The Monastic Way*, that we have countless facts about poor children and about families who have no homes, health care, or insurance. We know there are people who go to bed hungry every night. In the face of this, she challenges, "Where is the passion that turns the birth of Jesus into the life of Jesus?" Reading her words, I am compelled to remind myself that it was Christ's passionate love that made his Passion possible. Chittister continues: "We need a passion for life, a surge of gratitude, so deep that we will do whatever it takes to guarantee the fullness of life for the entire world."

Further on she writes:

> Whatever you do, do it with passion. Otherwise, why do it at all? . . . Passion is not pallid and not dour. Passion is what gives meaning to what seems meaningless, energy to what seems impossible, direction to what is scattered.[27]

Passion's great need is to be directed and focused and appropriately used. To kill passion is to mute the life force. I cannot help but pray, "God give us passion! Give us passion for you, passion for people, passion for meaning, and passion for life!"

CREATION, RESURRECTION, AND RE-CREATION

Out of chaos God brought ordered beauty. Out of utter darkness came life-giving light. Out of the first tiny, insignificant seed, a tree. Out of a sperm and egg, a person. Out of Sarah's old and barren womb, a son. Out of a nation of former slaves, a savior whose life has changed the world. Out of a tiny band of followers, a church that spans the earth.

God's way of bringing life out of nothing, blessing out of devastation, and hope out of hopelessness, sometimes bursts forth suddenly as an unrelenting force. But more often it arrives quietly and gradually, growing patiently and unperceived from the very heart of things. Life is as likely to grow from the inside out as to come from the outside in. God can work in either direction. God gives the gift. Faith receives without seeing. Tagore, the great twentieth-century poet of India, once wrote, "Faith is a bird that feels the light and sings when the dawn is still dark."[28]

It sings in us when we read the words: "For it is the God who said, 'Let light shine out of darkness,' who has shone in our hearts" (2 Corinthians 4:6). And it sings through the words of Isaiah, the prophet of hope:

> Do not remember the former things,
> or consider the things of old.
> I am about to do a new thing;
> now it springs forth, do you not perceive it?
> I will make a way in the wilderness
> and rivers in the desert . . .
> to give drink to my chosen people,
> the people I formed for myself
> so that they might declare my praise. (43:18-21)

Nothing is so pervasive in Scripture as the theme of resurrection, of new life, of hope for the future. It is not a naive point of view, ignoring suffering and pain. Instead it confronts that vivid reality with a greater reality that is above all others, an eternal truth.

Lecturing on the wilderness story in Deuteronomy, Luther uttered some of his most inspiring words about the God who transforms:

> He is willing and able to turn a rock into your drink, a desert into your food, nakedness into beautiful clothing, poverty into wealth, death into life, shame into glory, evil into good, enemies into friends.[29]

And we could add: water into wine, sickness into health, and earth into the kingdom of God! This is the God "who gives life to the dead and calls into existence the things that do not exist" (Romans 4:17).

We have been chosen to be involved in God's own saving purpose. In simple words, Teresa of Avila explains the divine plan:

> Christ has
> No body now on earth but yours;
> No hands but yours;
> No feet but yours;
> Yours are the eyes
> Through which [Christ's compassion
> looks out on] the world;
> Yours are the feet
> With which he is to go about
> Doing good;
> Yours are the hands
> With which he is to bless now.[30]

Our lives are "caught up in the holy labor of love through which God gives life to the world."[31]

We have been called to a task that seems impossible. And yet God speaks through Paul to say, "My grace is sufficient for you, for power is made perfect in weakness." (2 Corinthians 12:9) No wonder we can respond, "Whenever I am weak, then I am strong" (2 Corinthians 12:9-10). "I can do all things through [the Lord] who strengthens me" (Philippians 4:13). It is God's "power at work within us [which] is able to accomplish abundantly far more than all we can ask or imagine" (Ephesians 3:20).

DISCIPLES WHO BECAME APOSTLES: THOSE "SENT OUT"

The disciples whom Jesus addressed in that last meal together watched, we are told, as he ascended into heaven. Barbara Brown Taylor speaks words of life to you and me about that happening:

> No one standing around watching them that day could have guessed what an astounding thing happened when they all stopped looking into the sky and looked at each other instead.
>
> On the surface, it was not a great moment: eleven abandoned disciples with nothing to show for all their following. But in

the days and years to come it would become very apparent what had happened to them. With nothing but a promise and a prayer, those eleven people consented to become the church and nothing was ever the same again, beginning with them. The followers became leaders, the listeners became preachers, the converts became missionaries, the healed became healers. The disciples became apostles, witnesses of the risen Lord by the power of the Holy Spirit. . . .

Surprising things began to happen. They began to say things that sounded like him [Jesus] and they began to do things they had never seen anyone but him do before. They became brave and capable and wise. . . .

Why do you stand looking up toward heaven? Look around, look around![32]

THE COMMITTED HEART

STAKING OUR LIVES ON THE ONE WE TRUST

"Just as there is no fire without heat and smoke, so there is no faith without love," said Luther.[1] Faith is not only yes, but the yes of the heart. The issue in life is not who we become or what we possess or achieve. The issue is whom or what we love and what we will do for that love. It is what we are willing to stand for, to live for, and even to die for. It is not apart from our other treasures: our loved ones, our home, our dreams, and our own well-being. Rather it is what gives meaning and value to them all.

To trust gives us security. To love gives us life. If we can trust what we love and our trust is well-founded, we will have the strength to live.

Love without trust has no foundation and will not last unless it is compassionate, merciful love. Compassionate love is given for someone simply because that person is in need. It is God's life-giving love: *agape*, expecting nothing in return. It is not a covenantal relationship in which both parties commit to each other.

Trust without love may simply be admiration or dependency. It receives without an impulse to give back. It does not offer itself in response. It has no cost. It is not a part of covenant or commitment.

When Luther pledged his heart in trust, it was to the one to whom he owed his life, to the Lord of goodness and grace who had captured his heart. It was a response to the one who claims each one of us, not because we deserve it, but simply because we are cherished. Well might he have written the thoughts that some say were penned

153

by St. Francis Xavier, his contemporary. They focus on the love of God as known through Jesus:

> How can I choose but love thee, God's dear Son,
> O Jesus, loveliest and most loving one!
> Were there no heav'n to gain, no hell to flee,
> For what thou art alone I must love thee.
>
> Not for the hope of glory or reward,
> But even as thyself has loved me, Lord,
> I love thee, and will love thee and adore,
> Who art my King, my God, forevermore.[2]

Jesus has become the compelling focus of the lives of so many because in him the incredible love of God is seen, known, and felt. The crucifixion speaks to us of that unbelievable love above all else. It was lived out, made incarnate, put in terms we could understand and experience in order that we might know God intimately, might see and touch holiness in the midst of ordinary life.

When we are touched by this revelation of the holy in the ordinary, we yearn to respond in some adequate way. But there is none. We simply offer what we can. That was the plight of Martin Luther's beloved Bernard of Clairvaux to whom the original text of "O Sacred Head" is attributed:

> What language shall I borrow
> to thank Thee, dearest friend,
> for this, thy dying sorrow,
> thy pity without end?
> O make me thine forever,
> and, should I fainting be,
> O let me never, never
> outlive my love to Thee.[3]

Once again we see the simple truth: we love the one who first loved us. Each of us, now and always, is wrapped in the love of God.

Editor John Mogabgab writes in *Weavings* that our commitment is possible only because of God's original commitment to us.

> In time's infancy, an original act of divine love brought forth a human creature swaddled in divine commitment. So completely was God given to this creature, so fully did God perceive it as an intrinsic part of the divine life, that God etched

the mark of that life deep in its being. God's committed love abides at the core of human being. God's loving commitment sustains the foundation of human existence.[4]

Commitment is at the core of the covenant between God and human beings. Without commitment from both sides, there is no covenant, only a tentative agreement. Thus commitment is the basis for the solemn vow, the pledge, the oath, the promise that a covenant is. It is something "worthy of the whole heart," says Mogabgab. The faithfulness of God and human beings to each other is far more than "mere obligation and dogged willpower." Commitment is our yes, our joyous receptivity to God's eternal love, which has always come before our own was born.

Commitment is really another word for faithfulness, devotion, dedication, and consecration. It involves the whole self and influences one's whole life. The commitment that we speak of here is dedication to something greater than our own needs and well-being. It is living with a vision, a dream of a more loving, selfless world and doing something about it.

Commitment is caring with passion. It is a statement of faith. It is living what we believe and living for what we love. It truly is the yes of the heart. It can even be the fulfillment of God's dream for us, God's purpose for our lives, becoming who God has empowered us to be, doing what we believe we are meant to do.

One who is committed is willing to be an individual, with all that that means: to stand alone when necessary, to be responsible, to accept leadership or denigration, honor or exclusion.

Commitment is daring, risking, and caring because the goodness of life is so important that we cannot bear to have it imperceptibly slip into nonexistence.

Luther has some strong words about faithfulness within the church. He states: "The office of teaching in the church requires . . . a mind that despises all dangers." "All the devout should prepare themselves so that they are not afraid of becoming martyrs, that is, confessors or witnesses of God." How is that possible? Only the confirmation of the Spirit enables anyone to face such odds. The Spirit assures us of God's presence and God's firm will to save anyone willing to witness.[5]

God gives "three gifts of the Holy Spirit" or "three gifts of faith" says Luther: confidence in God's mercy, the presence of the Holy

Spirit who sanctifies us, and the strength to witness. We can count on God, we can sense the presence of the Holy Spirit as it brings us closer to God, and we are not afraid to say what we believe. These three are the basis for the yes of the heart, our commitment.[6]

Commitment gives energy and zest to our days. It brings us joy because it uses all we have and are. Commitment lives on hope, on faith, and on love. Without them, it cannot exist. They are its very strength. God gives them, and we give them to each other.

Revisiting Fowler in the Light of Commitment

When one looks at Fowler in the light of commitment, his final stage seems to deal with what we have been speaking of here. Fowler's stage six is commitment to something much greater than the self, something that is worth more than one's life. Fowler sees it as an expression of God's "divine intention to redeem, restore, and fulfill all being."[7]

Fowler's description of the deepest levels of commitment are similar to my own. But he calls stage six "exceedingly rare." I am not sure I agree with him about this.

Yes, the great souls among us *are* rare when compared with our confused, primarily self-centered society. But I have known scores of undiscovered saints, people whose unique individualities are as completely committed to God and neighbor as anyone could envision. They are those who, as Fowler puts it, live beyond obsessive concern for personal survival, security, or significance.[8]

Years ago, in the corner of my mother's bedroom mirror was tucked a poem by Catherine Herzel. It reminds me of such souls, people who recognize their inadequacies, yet love deeply and faithfully. The poem was titled "Disciples":

> Our feet may never feel the heat of Syrian sand,
> May never climb the stony slopes that saw Thee slain,
> May never joyful speed across a garden's green
> To tell some hopeless one that Thou dost live again.
>
> But, over other roads and places, other times,
> We walk, and in the dust ahead Thy footprints see,
> Disciples, too, though weak and slow to understand;
> And, oh! we stumble—but we rise to follow Thee.[9]

THE CHALLENGE OF INVOLVEMENT

It is easy to live on the edge of involvement because commitment costs so much. Only by experience do we learn that in attempting to help someone else heal, we may heal ourselves as well. Indifference is a shield against the invasion of compassion, compassion that steals away our complacency and leaves us vulnerable so that we feel another person's pain.

Last fall I preached a sermon titled "Who Is Lying at Our Door?" based on the story of the rich man and Lazarus (Luke 16:19-31). In the ten minutes before the service, I received two calls from people desperate for food, money, and medical attention. Every word I preached that day was a personal challenge to me. I knew I would be meeting with those sick and impoverished people when the service was over. And I wondered if I would express myself in the same way, should they enter while I was preaching.

I once asked someone to help another in an agonizing life situation, a man who belonged to the same church as did he. His reply was, "But I don't know him!" I realized later that I needed to encourage him by saying, "Our love must be greater than our fear!" There are times when to try to help others seems inappropriate or we feel inadequate because we do not know how to approach them. But when no one is doing anything and the situation is desperate, inappropriateness and even inadequacy are not the most important concerns. Physical and spiritual survival are. There are people dying because they have no one to care!

If we notice people whom others miss, we are surely called upon to help others see and feel for them. Rollo May, a psychotherapist, writes in *The Courage to Create*:

> Moral courage has its source in . . . identification . . . with the suffering of one's fellow human beings. . . . It depends on one's capacity to perceive, to let one's self see the suffering of other people. If we let ourselves experience the evil, we will be forced to do something about it. . . . [W]hen we don't want to . . . come to the aid of someone who is being unjustly treated, we block off our perception, we blind ourselves to the other's suffering, we cut off our empathy with the person needing help. Hence the most prevalent form of cowardice in our day hides behind the statement "I did not want to become involved."[10]

When we fear to be committed, we lose the ability to love. We may need love desperately and seek it endlessly. Yet we may have no sense of the amazing power of our own love to change the life of another. It is strange and wonderful that we can sometimes give to others what we yearn for but cannot give to ourselves.

Those who inspire us most, who give us strength, are those who "lose their lives" in giving life and, in the process, find their own lives full to overflowing. They dare to dream of a just and transformed world. They live for what is not yet but *could* and should be. They yearn for and they "see" what is possible although not yet actual. They live passionately, sometimes painfully, often joyously. They are faithful, persistent, even doggedly determined. They are impelled by a fire in their hearts and a vision in their minds. They can feel what another feels.

When one's friends or family beg, "Don't do it! It's not worth it! There will only be suffering and there will be no gain!" it is very difficult to say, "But perhaps this is why I am alive. Perhaps this is my unique gift to give. I think it is my call."

Self-doubt often appears when one decides to take such an individualistic course. It is easy to remember Elijah, alone in the wilderness and crying out to God, "It is enough! Now, O Lord, take away my life, for I am no better than my ancestors" (1 Kings 19:4)!

Robert Coles of Harvard speaks of the depths of this kind of pain:

> To stand outside the gates of money and power and rank and approved success and applause, to be regarded as irregular or odd or "sick" or, that final exile, as a traitor—such an outcome, in this era, carries its own special burdens and demands: the disapproval, if not derision, of colleagues, neighbors, the larger world of commentators who meticulously fall in line with reigning authority, but perhaps most devastating of all, the sense of oneself that is left in one's mind at the end of a day. What am I trying to do—and is this, after all, not only futile, but evidence that I have somehow gone astray?[11]

Hebrew scripture calls such people "prophets." They are those who will stick out their necks to criticize what needs to be changed: institutions, values, customs, laws, theologies. Often they are considered threats to those in power, and attempts are made to discredit or undermine them if they cannot be effectively ignored. They make us angry and uncomfortable. And we need them desperately!

Sometimes one of them will inspire us. Saints or heroes, we want to be like them, to do something that really helps, that deeply matters. We may forget that we have been called not to be heroes but to be God's salt upon the earth.

Ordinary, common, pervasive salt is found in the oceans that cover two-thirds of the world and in the soil that covers the rest. It is found in our food, and, as a warm-hearted woman in our congregation reminded me, it is found in our tears and in our perspiration. It flavors, preserves, heals, and in rock-salt form, it melts ice.

Jesus did not say that *some* people are his salt or that a special group of "the elect" would be chosen for that task. He said to all those who heard the Sermon (or sermons) on the Mount: "You are the salt of the earth." That means that all of us are called to give people the hope that flavors life and the strength that would keep the world from rotting! All of us are called to provide the purifying effect of an antiseptic and a compassion warm enough to melt ice.

But salt sitting in a salt cellar does not satisfy. It is useless unless it is sprinkled where it is needed. It is supposed to be spread around. It is the salt "of the earth!"

There is a story about Mao Tse-tung, the Communist leader of China from 1949 to 1976. Mao was once alarmed to discover a whole village full of Christians, so he scattered its inhabitants throughout the country. Years later the number of Christian villages had greatly multiplied. Each family from the original location had converted their new neighbors!

We may well be reminded of Joseph's statement to his brothers: "Even though you intended to do harm to me, God intended it for good" (Genesis 50:20)! When Luther preached on John 15:1, he commented about God pruning us and said something quite similar: "This is the purpose suffering serves . . . : God converts the wrath into an instrument working for their best." He explains further:

> God is a Master who can cause what would hinder and harm us to further and profit us; whatever would kill us, to serve to bring us to life; what would move us to sin and condemn us, to strengthen our faith and hope and to cause our prayer to be all the more effective and all the more richly answered.[12]

In *Life Together*, Dietrich Bonhoeffer makes a comment about Christians who are scattered throughout the world by God:

> It is not simply to be taken for granted that the Christian has the privilege of living among other Christians. Jesus Christ lived in the midst of his enemies. . . . So the Christian, too, belongs not in the seclusion of a cloistered life but in the thick of foes. There is his commission, his work.[13]

Then Bonhoeffer quotes Luther's needling comments:

> The Kingdom is to be in the midst of your enemies. And he who will not suffer this does not want to be of the Kingdom of Christ; he wants to be among friends, to sit among roses and lilies, not with the bad people but the devout people. O you blasphemers and betrayers of Christ! If Christ had done what you are doing who would ever have been spared?[14]

To all those who sometimes languish for lack of understanding and appreciation, encouragement, and support, those brusque words can bring tremendous encouragement. Sometimes we miss the importance of the seemingly insignificant and small. Yet Jesus did not. He spoke of the difference just a little salt could make, of the power in a grain of mustard seed, of a little leaven in one lump, of the light of one candle. He dared to begin his mission with only a group of twelve.

THE COST OF DISCIPLESHIP

When I took my first job as minister of music and youth work in a large Lutheran church in Madison, Wisconsin, one scriptural passage challenged and sustained me. It was the wonderful text of Philippians 3:7-12, where Paul writes of letting go of everything except the one who has grasped him in love and made him his own. It is important to quote it again:

> Yet whatever gains I had, these I have come to regard as loss because of Christ. More than that, I regard everything as loss because of the surpassing value of knowing Christ Jesus my Lord. For his sake I have suffered the loss of all things, and I regard them as rubbish, in order that I may gain Christ and be found in him. . . . I want to know Christ and the power of his resurrection and the sharing of his sufferings by becoming like

him in his death. . . . Not that I have already obtained this or have already reached the goal; but I press on to make it my own, because Christ Jesus has made me his own.

To me, those words mean that nothing matters in comparison to Christ. It took me years to realize that everything that does matter, matters because it belongs to God and is meant to be God's vessel.

Much later I came across a prayer of Charles de Foucauld, a Christian contemplative presence in the Muslim world. It too spoke to me. It taught me. But most of all it changed me as I prayed it:

> Father, I abandon myself into thy hands. Do with me as thou wilt. For whatever thou doest I thank thee. I am ready for all, I accept all. Let only thy will be done in me as in all thy creatures, and I will ask nothing else, my Lord. Into thy hands I commend my soul; I give it thee, Lord, with the love of my heart. For I love thee, my God, and so need to give, to surrender myself into thy hands with a trust beyond all measure because thou art my Father.[15]

That absolute surrender, that "abandonment to God" also speaks out through Bonhoeffer's *The Cost of Discipleship*. We have noted his words earlier: "When Christ calls a man, he bids him to come and die."[16] In another lecture, he had made an even more startling statement: "Either man must die, or he kills Jesus"![17] Surely he means that either we let go of our self-centeredness (the root of all estrangement and all sin) or we will become part of those forces that conspire against the work of Christ, against the healing of the earth. Unless we die to our innate selfishness, we become part of the spirit that killed Jesus.

In 1934, a year after Hitler was made chancellor of Germany, Bonhoeffer dared to help organize the Confessing Church, "a critical response" both to the regime and to his own traditional Lutheran church. He taught in the underground seminary in Finkenwalde. In 1937, the seminary was closed by the Gestapo, but his book *The Cost of Discipleship* was published.

Just two years later, Bonhoeffer returned to Union Theological Seminary in New York City, where nine years before he had been a Sloan Fellow for a year. This time he remained for only five weeks. To the dismay of his American friends, he turned his face toward his homeland much as Jesus turned his toward Jerusalem. His colleagues considered it insane, reckless, and unreasonable. But Bonhoeffer gave his reason clearly in a letter to Reinhold Niebuhr:

> I shall have no right to participate in the reconstruction of Christian life in Germany after the war if I do not share the trials of this time with my people. . . . . Christians in Germany will face the terrible alternative of either willing the defeat of their nation in order that Christian civilization may survive, or willing the victory of their nation . . . . thereby destroying our civilization. I know which of these alternatives I must choose; but I cannot make this choice in security.[18]

He could not choose security over the loving obedience that he called "discipleship." So he returned and became a double agent in the *Abwehr*, the Military Intelligence.

Robert Coles notes that "within days of Hitler's ascension as chancellor, Bonhoeffer spoke up, took on Nazism as idolatrous, spoke in defense of the Jews, and warned strenuously against the direction his nation was going." He was cut off in the middle of his radio address.[19]

But even at the young age of twenty-two, Bonhoeffer was choosing what was most important in life. He was curate then to a congregation in Spain. In an address there he said:

> Christ has, in effect, been eliminated from our lives. Of course, we build him a temple, but we live in our own houses. Christ has become a matter of the church or rather, of . . . churchiness . . . not a matter of life. . . . However one thing is clear: we understand Christ only if we commit ourselves to him in a stark "Either-Or. . . . If we wish to have him, then he demands the right to say something decisive about our entire life. . . . [He asks:] 'Will you follow me wholeheartedly or not at all?' . . . The religion of Christ is not a tidbit after one's bread; on the contrary, it is bread or it is nothing.[20]

Christ's claim was always absolute for Bonhoeffer. But Hitler's rise to power in 1933 made it crucial. Then he realized clearly that, in his time and place, the commitment he called "discipleship" must be lived out in the heart of the world, not in a rarefied, supposedly spiritual atmosphere and not within consecrated but secluded walls. In one of his last letters from prison before his execution, he asked whether a real follower of Christ should not abandon religion and follow Christ instead! He wondered whether true followers should be "religionless-secular" Christians. Freed from religiosity, they would more truly be "those who are called forth" (as the church was supposed to be and as its name, in Greek, implies). Those "called forth" should be those "belonging wholly to the world," that is, living in the heart of the world and bringing it Christ's life.[21]

Bonhoeffer criticized the church. He claimed it taught God's redemptive grace but what cost God so much was received all too easily by uninvolved and uncommitted Christians. They ignored the unavoidable cost of commitment. They had forgotten that the church had been built on the blood of Christians. Bonhoeffer was obviously saying that commitment, like covenant, has two sides: God's and ours. God gives in grace; we receive in faith, and that faith compels us to pass on what we have received.

In *The Cost of Discipleship* Bonhoeffer writes:

> Cheap grace is the preaching of forgiveness without requiring repentance, baptism without church discipline, Communion without confession, absolution without personal confession. Cheap grace is grace without discipleship, grace without the cross, grace without Jesus Christ, living and incarnate.[22]

To receive God's grace, to surrender to it, says Bonhoeffer, will cost us everything. But we do not want to hear that. While our abstract theology can exist safely removed from personal obedience, it offers only a "Christianity without the living Christ." It is "Christianity without discipleship."[23]

Along with his two brothers-in-law and Klaus, his brother, Bonhoeffer plotted and attempted the unsuccessful overthrow of Hitler. The consequence, on April 5, 1943, was his imprisonment. It lasted two years. On April 9, 1945, just a month before the end of World War II, he became, by special order, one of the very last of the twelve million victims of the Holocaust. That terrible destruction had taken six million Jews and six million non-Jews, many of them friends who had hidden and supported the Jewish population. They were the noble, mostly unknown souls willing to sacrifice for the preservation of true humanity and for their country as they believed it was called to be.

Bonhoeffer lived what he believed, and he even found joy in the concentration camp. He wrote to his fiancée, Maria von Wedemeyer, from prison:

> No evil can befall us: whatever men may do to us, they cannot but serve the God who is secretly revealed as love and rules the world and our lives. We must learn to say: 'I know how to be abased and how to abound.' . . . I can do all things through him who strengthens me (Philippians 4:12-13). . . . What is meant here is not stoical resistance . . . , but true endurance and true rejoicing in the knowledge that Christ is with us.[24]

For Bonhoeffer, although discipleship costs, it is a magnificent privilege. He wrote, "Grace is costly because it costs a man his life, and it is grace because it gives a man the only true life."[25]

THE COURAGE OF COMMITMENT

Evelyn Underhill comments wryly in *The Ways of the Spirit*, "It is a very poor sort of faith and love that will not face a dark passage until it knows where the switch is!"[26]

The book of Hebrews comments much more seriously: "Faith is the assurance of things hoped for, a conviction of things not seen" (11:1). Although we are touched by grace, a reality that intimates there is always more, we realize that it cannot yet be fully known. We know that our courage does not come from clear-sightedness, from a thundering call of God, from complete revelation. We recognize that it comes from touches of God upon our lives, from the warmth of God in others, from the belief that where this came from, there is more.

In the same vein, Rollo May writes, "To live into the future means to leap into the unknown and this requires a degree of courage . . . which few people realize."[27] Commitment necessarily requires courage at some point, but courage, in turn, has no strength to exist without commitment.

Nevertheless, the yes that centers our lives will always be challenged. May continues: "We must be fully committed, but we must also be aware at the same time that we might possibly be wrong." Obviously he means that the courage of commitment needs to be firm but not inflexible, not close-minded. Courage needs to allow an openness to what is "not yet." May adds:

Commitment is healthiest when it is not *without* doubt, but *in spite of* doubt. To believe fully and at the same moment to have doubts is not at all a contradiction: it presupposes a greater respect for truth, an awareness that truth always goes beyond anything that can be said or done at any given moment.[28]

Perhaps May's most inspiring insight is that "courage is not the absence of despair" but "the capacity to move ahead in spite of despair," in spite of depression, in spite of hopelessness.[29]

The "act of nevertheless" is not just one of determination but of surrender. It is in our weakness that we are made strong, in our depending that we can be filled.

Evelyn Underhill, writing on courage, speaks of surrender: "However hard we will to be [God's] agents, it doesn't come off that way. It only comes by way of surrender of the whole human person to His purposes. And to be able to make that willing surrender, to say yes to God, is the most solemn dynamic of Gethsemane."

One of Underhill's recurring themes is that "true Christianity is not all beauty and calm." She writes, "In one form or another, it will involve that awful question [posed by Jesus], 'Can you drink the cup I drink of?' (Matthew 20:22)." The inspiring, exciting side of commitment can easily be lost. One may have to drink "drop by drop out of a tin mug . . . the wine of the surrendered life."[30]

The great fear in almost all of us is to lose our life. That fear comes in many guises. The early twentieth-century psychologist Otto Rank taught that men in particular have a "death fear" of losing their independence and becoming totally absorbed by another individual. In contrast, Rank also perceived a "life fear" in women: a fear of abandonment, a fear to face autonomous living, a fear to attempt self-actualization. Such a fear can be dangerous because the woman, who has been taught to be devoted, can throw herself so completely into a relationship that she has no self left. In both cases there is a challenge to be oneself while still being concerned, becoming involved, and participating in the lives of others.[31]

There is also a challenge for both the young and the old. The young person wants as much of life as she or he can get. The old may be tempted to "retire" from life in general, just attending to his or her own wants and needs, forgetting that all of us can be vessels of God until we die if we only have the imagination to see how.

If the reason for our lives is to learn to love, to give life, then as long as we breathe, we have some of that ability. May writes that creative people can bring life and hope and relief. They can bring "form amidst discord, beauty amidst ugliness, and some human love in the midst of hatred." It is a gift that reaches even beyond their death.[32]

HOPE: IMAGINING THE "NOT YET"

Hope is not an optimism that denies the truth but a way of facing reality and finding a life-giving means to deal with it. Jesuit William F. Lynch offers three paths for looking toward the future: *imagining what is possible, depending on supportive friendship, and learning the grace of waiting until the future becomes actual.*[33] I would like to give my own response to these.

Nothing will ever be that is not imagined—either by God, by another, or by ourselves. Imagination precedes all that we do, even crossing a room. We must imagine every action before it can be accomplished. It is an error to think of imagination as frivolous, unreal, or unimportant. Without it, language would not exist, for words are symbols of pictures in our minds. Every great invention and every important social movement has been imagined before it has become fact. In receptive prayer (the prayer of trust) we receive God's guidance, often through a picture of what could or ought to be. All consecrated art is an imaging, a projecting, in color, form, sound, or movement of a deeper level of awareness. Both sin and blessing result from this gift. We cannot function without imagination. We cannot hope without it.

Hope is made possible by the support of other people. At the very moment I am writing, someone I know is on the edge of death because she has lost hope. And she has lost hope because she has lost her home and all her possessions, she has lost her health, and long ago, she lost the normal functioning of her mind. I am convinced that if others would show her love, her sense of worth might be revived, her hope might be renewed, and she might live meaningfully, hanging on to the God of hope in almost every breath.

It is amazing that we can go through almost anything if someone goes with us. This is much of the power of the Twenty-third Psalm. The Shepherd goes with us through almost every line. It is clearest of all when the Psalmist says: "Yea, though I walk through the valley of the shadow of death, I will fear no evil, for thou art with me." God is wherever we are, wherever that is, even if we don't know where that is! We are told it over and over. "I will not leave you or forsake you" (Hebrews 13:5). "With long life I will satisfy [you], and show [you] my salvation" (Psalm 91:16). "Remember, I am with you always, even to the end of the age" (Matthew 28:20). We can survive if we are not alone. We can even hope.

But yes, we must *wait* for "the fullness of time," for the coincidence of our own imagining, the support of others, hanging on while growing in God. Only with confidence, with trust, do we have the strength for some trials, for what seems endless waiting. Faith calls us to hope, and hope rests on faith. We cannot live without hope.

Many of us have been close to despair, yet we have survived. How is that possible? Surely it is because we can at least remember the touch of Someone who is stronger and more far-seeing than we are, Someone who knows what life is all about and is aware of where the world is going, Someone to whom we belong for all eternity, Someone who hangs on to us when it is so hard to hope.

In the hours, days, and years ahead, there are people in this world who will know the greatest desperation a human being can face, who will be pared down by deprivation to the core of their being, yet still have hope, and why? Because there is a life that supports and transcends the facts of their earthly existence. There are those who will someday be washed clean of everything but the most essential nub of life, where all that is left is the flame of God's life burning within their hearts. These are those who will say with Paul and Bonhoeffer: "Whether we live or whether we die, we are the Lord's" (Romans 14:8).

We can live and we can die for God. We do live or die in God, in God's presence, whether we realize it or not. What is real is more than we can see and far more than we have experienced. "No eye has seen, nor ear heard, nor has the human heart conceived, what God has prepared for those who love him" (1 Corinthians 2:9).

Because God will always be where I am, I can be where God is. "Though the earth should change, though the mountains shake in the heart of the sea, though its waters roar and foam, . . . God is in our midst . . ." (Psalm 46:2-3, 5). And we are in God.

Julian of Norwich lived in the midst of the Black Plague of the fourteenth century. Healthy people came daily to her cell and many were dead by nightfall. Yet Julian is best known for proclaiming, "But all will be well, and every kind of thing will be well."[34]

The author of Hebrews notes that we are encouraged to "seize the hope set before us" (Hebrews 6:18). A life of hope is a life of repentance in the most positive sense: of turning around and facing a new direction. A life of hope is focusing not on the problem but on the solution, not on loss but on what needs to be done, not on the past but on the present and future, not on death but on life. Hope calls us to an intentional focus on what is possible and potential, on allowing grace to grasp us in our lives.

As a little girl I discovered Marion Anderson, her voice, and her spirit. She became my hero. Probably from the scriptures she had taken words and thoughts that she put together in her own way. I remember memorizing them: "I have opened my mouth to the Lord and I will not turn back. I will go, I shall go to see what the end will be!"

Without that kind of hope, Luther could not have told us what trust is all about: "Faith is the yes of the heart, a confidence on which one stakes one's life!"

Saying "Yes"

We do not say yes to God without a reason, and the reasons have filled the pages of this book. We have been loved to life. We can love because we were loved first. We are the result of the creative, life-giving love of God, a love that knew us in the womb and has always nourished and challenged, called and guided us. Our answer to that call is our own self-offering.

That offering asks us to let go of all that stands between us and God. It asks us to live what we believe. It asks us to abide, to hang on, to trust in darkness and in light. And when the night comes, we learn that we are not alone, that God knows our confusion and shares our pain but sees beyond, for "darkness is as light" to the one who created both.

We may well discover that God can even use the passion of our grief in a new, life-giving way. We may come to experience "growth in grace," a renewal and an increase of the gift of the Holy Spirit. Eventually we may accept ourselves as vessels intended to hold and to share the life of God with those whose struggle becomes our own. Then we may learn the cost of commitment and the privilege of discipleship.

Then we may discover that all that has transpired, all that has been asked of us and all that we have been given by grace, has led to more than surrender and sacrifice. It has led to fulfillment, to doing, in some measure, what we were called to do. It has given life meaning, and we are grateful.

Paul Tillich taught that yes and no form "the law of all life" and vie with each other throughout our days. One no can cancel yes. Despair can extinguish hope. Death puts out life. But there is a larger reality that touches us to tell us there is more. There is resurrection! We taste it even in time. We can endure the temporal conflict of yes and no because, even now, "we participate in the Yes beyond . . . because we are in it, and it is in us." We live in the Eternal Now. We are participants of the Resurrection! "[T]herefore, we can say the ultimate Yes, the Amen beyond our Yes and our No." We can say the ultimate yes because God is ours and we are God's forever.[35]

I wonder if Tillich knew the simple words of Augustine as he looked beyond his finite days:

All shall be Amen and Alleluia.
We shall rest and we shall see,
We shall know and we shall love.
We shall love and we shall praise.
Behold our end which is no end.[36]

Luther would surely respond,"This is most certainly true."

Amen.

Yes!

Endnotes

1. Martin Luther, "Sermon for the Sunday after the Feast of the Circumcision, January 4, 1540," "Weimar Edition" *(WA),* vol. 49, p. 9. This statement, on which the title of this book is based, is as follows in the original: "*Fides ist ein herzlich jawort, das drauff stirbt.*" It may be translated: "Faith is a heartfelt confidence (conviction, or affirmation) for which one would die." The translation used in this book is similar to that found in the collection *What Luther Says* (Concordia Publishing House, 1959), which translates it: "Faith is the yes of the heart, a conviction on which one stakes one's life."

Introduction

1. Martin Luther, "The Freedom of a Christian" in *Three Treatises* (Philadelphia: Fortress Press, 1960), 288; hereafter referred to as Luther, "Freedom." "The Latin term *fides* meant both belief in God and trust in God or commitment, but Luther tried to strengthen the second understanding by referring to his "faith of the heart" as *fides fiducialis.* (Karl Barth and others have referred to this as *fiducia*, which actually means the same thing as *fides.*)" Professor Gerard S. Sloyan, in correspondence March 14, 1999. The Greek term *pistis* also embraces the concept of trust, confidence, obedience, a personal relationship to Christ, and belief in God's words. Gerhard Kittel and Gerhard Friedrich, *Theological Dictionary of the New Testament* 6:203–14.

2. Roland H. Bainton, *Here I Stand: A Life of Martin Luther* (Nashville: Abingdon Press, 1950), 49.

3. Joseph Sittler, *The Doctrine of the Word* (Philadelphia: Board of Publication, ULCA, 1948), 35–41n, 64, 68. Bengt Hoffman, *Luther and*

the Mystics (Minneapolis: Augsburg, 1976), 17–36; hereafter Sittler, *Doctrine*. John Dillenberger, *Protestant Christianity* (New York: Charles Scribner's Sons, 1988), 85, 89, 97, 98, 122–23. Tuomo Mannermaa, "Justification and Theosis in Lutheran-Orthodox Perspective" in *Union with Christ: The New Finnish Interpretation of Luther* (Grand Rapids, Mich.: William B. Eerdmans Publishing Company, 1998), 25–27.

4. From a conversation with Tom Williamson January 5, 1994. See his book *Attending Parishioners' Spiritual Growth* (Washington, D.C.: Alban Institute, 1997).

5. Brame, Grace Adolphsen. *Capacity for God: Evelyn Underhill's Theology of Spirituality*. Intro. (manuscript in preparation)

1. Faith: Saying Yes from the Heart

1. Martin Luther, *Lectures on Galatians,* (1535) in *Luther's Works*, ed. Jaroslav Pelikan and Helmut T. Lehman (St. Louis: Concordia Publishing House, and Philadelphia: Fortress Press, joint publishers), 26:129, 130; hereafter referred to as *LW*.

2. Martin Luther, "Preface to the Epistle of St. Paul to the Romans, 1522" in *Martin Luther: Selections from His Writings*, ed. John Dillenberger (New York: Anchor Books, Doubleday & Company, Inc. 1961), 26.

3. Also see Isaiah 45:7, Psalm 51:8, Lamentations 3:8, Amos 3:6, Isaiah 6:10.

4. Martin Luther, "Weimar Edition" *LW* 49:9 in *What Luther Says: An Anthology*, comp. Ewald M. Plass (St. Louis: Concordia Publishing Co., 1959), 467; hereafter referred to as *W*.

5. Evelyn Underhill, *The Ways of the Spirit*, comp., ed., and intro. by Grace Adolphsen Brame (New York: Crossroad, 1990), 214.

6. Martin Luther, letter to the Cardinal Archbishop of Mainz, July 6, 1530, in *What Luther Says*, 477 #1409; *W* 30 II:400.

7. *Encyclopedia Judaica* (Jerusalem: Macmillan Co., 1971), 803, 804; hereafter referred to as *Judaica*. Also *The Interpreter's Dictionary of the Bible* (New York: Abingdon Press, 1962), 105.

8. Martin Luther, *Commentaries on the Psalms* in *LW* 12:379. The etymological appendix to the *American Heritage Dictionary* notes *kerd, heart*, probably comes from a root also meaning "to place trust," which is also the source for the word *credence* or *belief.* See Third Edition, 1992 (Boston: Houghton Mifflin), 2108.

9. *The Jewish Encyclopedia*, ed. Isidore Singer (New York: Ktav Publishing House, 1976), 6:295–97.

10. Abraham Joshua Heschel, *Quest for God* (New York: Crossroad, 1987), 12–14, 37–40. Heschel writes of *kavanah*, referring to one's intention, purpose, and devotion in worship. Medieval Jews would say, "Prayer without kavanah is like the body without a soul." Thus form without the heart's involvement has no meaning.

11. *Service Book and Hymnal of the Lutheran Church in America* (Minneapolis: Augsburg Publishing House, and Philadelphia: Board of Publication, Lutheran Church in America, 1958), #150; hereafter referred to as *SBH*.

2. Born from the Heart of God

1. *Psalms with Introductions by Martin Luther*, intro. and trans. Bruce A. Cameron (St. Louis: Concordia, 1993), 178.

2. *Sermons of Martin Luther*, ed. J. N. Lenker (Grand Rapids, Mich.: Baker, 1905, 1995 ed.), 5:178, 180; hereafter referred to as *Sermons/Postils*.

3. Ibid., 5:182.

4. Ibid., 3:291.

5. *Commentary on the Magnificat* (1521), *LW* 21:309.

6. See chapter 8, dealing with God's relationship to us in our suffering.

7. Underhill, *Ways*, 229.

8. Meister Eckhart, *Meister Eckhart: Sermons*, trans. Raymond B. Blakney (New York: Harper & Row, 1941), 129; hereafter referred to as Eckhart.

9. *What Luther Says*, n. 6, 824.

10. Ibid., 986, based on *Lectures on Romans 8:3* (1516); but see also *LW* 25:346.

11. *The Theologia Germanica*, comp., intro., and trans. Bengt Hoffman (New York: Paulist, 1980), 130–36; hereafter referred to as *Theologia*. The author of this quote is anonymous but is known to have been a priest in Frankfurt, Germany.

12. Note 4 above.

13. The well-known statement "*Simul iustus et peccator*," meaning "at the same time justified and sinful." In both *Lectures on Romans*, *WA* 56, 70, 272, and *Lectures on Galatians* (1519), *WA* 2, 496f.

14. Martin Luther, "A Brief Instruction on What to Look for and Expect in the Gospels," *LW* 35:121.

15. ———, Sermon on Mark 16:14–20, May 29, 1522, in *What Luther Says*, 477, #1410; *W* 10 III:139.

16. Martin Luther, "Preface to Romans," *LW* 35:371

17. Henri Nouwen, *The Return of the Prodigal Son* (New York: Doubleday Image Books, 1994; orig. 1992), 95.

18. The term for this concept is *panentheism*. *Pan* = all; *en* = in; *theos* = God. Thus, *all (is) in God*. It should never be confused with pantheism, which says everything is God, a heresy for Christianity.

19. Hildegard of Bingen in *Original Blessing* by Matthew Fox (Santa Fe: Bear and Co, 1984; orig. 1983), 89; hereafter referred to as Fox.

20. Olé Hallesby, *Prayer* (Minneapolis: Augsburg, 1994; orig. 1934), 13.

21. Rufus Jones in *A Guide to Prayer for Ministers and Other Servants*, ed. Reuben P. Job and Norman Shawchuck (Nashville: The Upper Room, 1983), 21; hereafter referred to as Reuben Job.

22. Martin Luther, *Devotional Writings*, LW 43:34, 35.

23. , *Lectures on Galatians* (1535), *LW* 26:167.

3. Christ Born in the Human Heart

1. Phillips Brooks, "O Little Town of Bethlehem" in *Lutheran Book of Worship* (Minneapolis: Augsburg, and Philadelphia: Board of Publication Lutheran Church in America, 1978), #41; hereafter referred to as *LBW*.

2. Timothy Richard Matthews, "Thou Didst Leave Thy Throne," *SBH*, #433.

3. This, an honorary title meaning "the angel of Silesia," was bestowed on Johannes Scheffler (1624–1677). See *Angelus Silesius: The Cherubic Wanderer*, trans. with foreword Marie Shrady (Mahwah, N.J.: Paulist Press, 1986).

4. Luther, "Freedom," 315. (See p. 59 here.)

5. Martin Luther, "This Child Is Sent to Fill Thine Heart." (I am told this is one of Luther's 1520 Christmas sermons, but it does not come from any of his Christmas sermons that I have seen. Perhaps it is apocryphal. I would appreciate information on this.)

6. Martin Luther, "From Heaven Above," *LBW* 51.

7. The Catholic ecumenicist Yves M. J. Congar, who influenced Vatican II theology so greatly, notes Hugo Rahner's work detailing the history of this concept. Congar's book is *The Word and the Spirit* (San Francisco: Harper & Row, 1986). Hugo Rahner's work is "Die Gottesgeburt" in *Symbole der Kirche. Die Ekklesiologie der Vater* (Salzburg, 1964), 11–87.

8. Eckhart, 96, 107, 119. See the first seven sermons particularly.

9. Martin Luther, Roerer's Notes (1550), based on *Luther's Lectures on Isaiah 53:11*. See *What Luther Says*, 470, #1387; *W* 40 III:737f.

10. Martin Luther, *The Martin Luther Christmas Book*, trans. and arr. by Roland H. Bainton (Philadelphia: The Muhlenberg Press, 1948), 44.

11. Grace Adolphsen Brame, *Receptive Prayer* (St. Louis: Chalice Press, 1985; first ed., Charis Enterprises, 1981); hereafter referred to as Brame, *Receptive Prayer*.

12. Martin Luther, "Sermon on the Afternoon of Christmas Day" on Luke 2:1–14 (1530), *LW* 51:214.

13. Ibid., 216.

14. Jared Wicks, S.J., "Martin Luther: The Heart Clinging to the Word" in *Spiritualities of the Heart*, Annice Callahan, R.S.C.J. (New York: Paulist, 1990), 79.

15. Johann B. Koenig, "On My Heart Imprint Thine Image," *The Lutheran Hymnal* (St. Louis: Concordia Publishing House, 1941), #179.

16. Martin Luther, Sermon on Galatians 4:1–5, given January 4, 1540, and, as far as I know, available only in medieval German and Latin. This is the same sermon from which the title of the book was taken. *W* 49:9.

17. Note paintings by Holman Hunt, Warner Sallman, and Heinrich Hoffmann.

18. *Theologia*, 63.

19. Martin Luther, *Lectures on Genesis*, *LW* 3:24.

4. Loving with Both Head and Heart

1. Professor Thomas Francis McDaniel, The Eastern Baptist Theological Seminary, Philadelphia, in conversation, June 1, 1998.

2. See Introduction, note 1.

3. Martin Buber, *Two Types of Faith* (London: Routledge & Kegan Paul Ltd., 1951), 7, 8.

4. Evelyn Underhill, *The Life of the Spirit and the Life of Today* (London: Methuen & Co. Ltd., 1928; first pub. 1922), 207.

5. Martin Luther, in a sermon based on Matthew 19:13–15, in *What Luther Says*, 485, #1440; *W* 47:328.

6. Paul Tillich, *Dynamics of Faith* (New York: Harper and Brothers Publishers, 1957), 44–48. (Hereafter, Tillich, *Dynamics*.)

7. James H. Fowler, *Stages of Faith* (San Francisco: HarperSanFrancisco, 1981), 119–213.

8. Thomas A. Droege, *Faith Passages and Patterns* (Philadelphia: Fortress Press, 1983), 79–80.

9. Sittler, *Doctrine*, 48,49.

10. Martin Luther, Letter to people in Frankfurt am Main (1532). See *What Luther Says*, 469, #1384.

11. ———, in a sermon on Luke 2:15–20, *LW* 52:32,33.

12. Tillich, *Dynamics*, 32.

13. *What Luther Says*, 471, #1391; *W* 10 III:306.

14. Luther, "Freedom," 280.

15. Luther, "Preface to Romans," 23.

16. Luther, "Freedom," 284.

17. Olivier Clement, *The Roots of Christian Mysticism* (New York: New City Press, 1995), 100–102.

18. Luther, "Freedom," 289, 315.

19. Augustine in *The Word and the Spirit* by Yves Congar (San Francisco: Harper & Row Publisher, 1986), 22.; hereafter Congar, *Word*.

20. Martin Luther, W*A* 7:546, in Congar, *Word*, 31.

21. ———, *Lectures on Isaiah*, *LW* 17:230. "To assent to that Word is the work of the Holy Spirit."

22. Quoted in Sittler, *Doctrine*, 25. Also see Sittler, 10.

23. In Congar, *Word*, 13.

24. Tillich, *Dynamics*, 41.

25. Richard P. McBrien, *Catholicism* (Minneapolis: Winston Press, 1981), 1258.

26. Focusing on the *Devotio Moderna* (see Gerhard Groote) and *Pietism* (see Jacob Spener and the Halle School especially). Paulist Press has volumes on both in their Western Spirituality Series.

27. Only three individuals have been officially named "theologians" by the Eastern Orthodox Church: St. Symeon the New Theologian, St. Gregory Nazianzen, and St. John of Damascus.

5. The Heart Called and Offered

1. Luther, *Lectures on Romans*, 33.

2. Martin Luther, *Lectures on Galatians* (1535), *LW* 26:172–75.

3. "*Without the grace of God*, the will produces an act that is perverse and evil" (emphasis added). Point 7 in "Disputation against Scholastic Theology," in *Martin Luther's Basic Theological Writings*, ed. Timothy F. Lull (Minneapolis: Fortress Press, 1989), 13.

4. Martin Luther, preaching on 1 John 4:16–21 in 1532 in *What Luther Says*, 819, #2540; *W* 36:424.

5. Underhill, *Ways*, 195.

6. *The Interpreter's Bible*, 802.

7. Martin Luther. Quoted in Paul Althaus, *The Theology of Martin Luther*, trans. Robert C. Schulz (Philadelphia: Fortress Press, 1966), 314, 315.

8. Martin Luther, *The Small Catechism: in Contemporary English* (Minneapolis: Augsburg, and Philadelphia: Fortress, 1979), 14.

9. Brame, *Receptive Prayer*.

10. Gerald G. Jampolsky, *Love Is Letting Go of Fear* (Millbrae, Calif.: Celestial Arts, 1979).

11. Tillich, *Dynamics*, 114.

12. George Matheson, "O Love That Will Not Let Me Go," *LBW*, #324. D. Macmillan, *The Life of George Matheson* (New York: A. C. Armstrong and Son, 1907), 181.

13. Ignatius of Loyola in Underhill, *Ways*, 122.

14. Frances Ridley Havergal, "Take My Life and Let It Be Consecrated," *SBH*, #510.

15. *LBW*, 67, 87.

16. Evelyn Underhill, *Worship* (New York: Harper & Brothers, 1936), 48.

17. Gordon Lathrop, *Holy Things: A Liturgical Theology* (Minneapolis: Fortress Press, 1993), 140.

18. Michael Barnes, *In the Presence of Mystery* (Mystic, Conn.: Twenty-third Publications, 1984), 18, 19.

19. Also see Amos 5:21, 24; Psalm 40:6; Psalm 50:12–14, 23.

20. Martin Luther, *The Suppression of the Private Mass*, *WA* 8, 468, 24 in Jared Wicks, *Luther and His Spiritual Legacy* (Wilmington, Del.: Michael Glazier, 1983), 128.

21. Martin Luther, *Lectures on Romans*, *LW* 25:435.

22. Augustine in Evelyn Underhill, *The Mystery of Sacrifice* (London: Longmans, Green and Co., 1938), 20.

23. "Take, O take me as I am" in *Come All You People*, composed principally by John L. Bell (Chicago: GIA Publications, 1994).

6. Choices of the Heart

1. See *William Wordsworth: The Prelude, Selected Poems and Sonnets*, intro. Carlos Baker (New York: Holt, Rinehart and Winston, 1954), 186.

2. Evelyn Underhill, *The Spiritual Life* (London: Hodder and Stoughton, 1937), 24.

3. Søren Kierkegaard, *Purity of Heart* (New York: Harper & Brothers, 1938), 99.

4. Dietrich Bonhoeffer, *The Cost of Discipleship* (New York: Macmillan, 1967), 99.

5. *Johannes Tauler: Sermons*, trans. Maria Shrady, intro. Josef Schmidt, and pref. Alois Haas (New York: Paulist Press, 1985), 31.

6. Regin Prenter, *Spiritus Creator* (Philadelphia: Fortress Press, 1953), 134.

7. Brame, *Receptive Prayer*, 107.

8. Also see Carl G. Jung, *The Undiscovered Self* (Boston: Little, Brown 1958).

9. Luther, "Freedom," 278.

10. Martin Luther, *Lectures on Galatians* (1519), *LW* 27:238.

11. Quoted in Dietrich Bonhoeffer's *Life Together*, trans. and intro. John W. Doberstein (San Francisco: HarperCollins, 1954), 77; hereafter Bonhoeffer, *Life*. See Bonhoeffer's comments on the self on the same page. From *LW* 35; 1:54.

12. Martin Luther, *Lectures on Genesis*, *LW* 5, 223.

13. Étienne de Grellet, Attribution. Not found in his writings. Also attributed to Emerson, Wesley, and Carlisle.

14. Bainton, *Here I Stand*, 67.

15. Dorothee Soelle and Shirley A. Cloyes, *To Work and to Love* (Philadelphia: Fortress Press, 1986; first ed. 1984), 72.

7. Abiding in God's Heart

1. Martin Luther, *Lectures on Romans*, *LW* 25:251.

2. *What Luther Says*, 1082, #3453; *W* 32:415.

3. Ibid., 1091, #3486; *W* 5 II:300.

4. Martin Luther, "A Simple Way to Pray," *Devotional Writings*. *LW* 43:193.

5. Hallesby, 36, 146, 147.

6. Bonhoeffer, *Life*, 87.

7. Hallesby, 115.

8. Wicks, *Heart*, 85.

9. *What Luther Says*, 1079, #3444; *W* 45:540.

10. Paul Tillich, "Spiritual Presence" in *The Eternal Now* (New York: Charles Scribner's Sons, 1963), 88, 89.

11. Ann Ulanov, *Primary Speech: A Psychology of Prayer* (Atlanta: J. Knox, 1982).

12. Harry Emerson Fosdick, *The Meaning of Prayer* (New York: Association Press, 1915), 87.

13. *What Luther Says*,1086, #3467; *W* 17 II:49.

14. Ibid., 1085, #3466; *W* 2:85.

15. Hallesby, 117.

16. Cynthia Hirni, "The Ridgeleaf" (Bangor, Pa.: Kirkridge Retreat Center, March 1992), #189.

17. Professor McDaniel, in conversation, September 1, 1999.

18. Underhill, *Ways*, 117.

19. Bonhoeffer, *Life*, 78, 79.

20. See "Prayerful Reading" in chapter 4 of this book and Brame, *Receptive Prayer*, 38.

21. Martin, Luther, Comment on John 1:5 in *Sermons on the Gospel of John, LW* 22:43.

22. *LW* 51:171. "On Prayer" in *Ten Sermons on the Catechism*. Compare Psalm 81:10: "Open your mouth wide and I will fill it."

23. See Ronald Klug. *How to Keep a Spiritual Journal* (Minneapolis: Augsburg Books, 1993). It is an excellent and useful guide.

24. "Apology of the Augsburg Confession" in *The Book of Concord*, trans. and ed. Theodore G. Tappert (Philadelphia: Fortress Press, 1959), 213.

8. The Suffering Heart

1. John Calvin, *Forms of Prayer for the Church*, 106. As quoted in Dorothee Soelle, *Suffering* (Philadelphia: Fortress Press, 1975), 24.

2. For instance, see Psalms 1 and 91 and Deuteronomy 30:15–20.

3. "Christians without a Prayer," *The Wall Street Journal*, Dec. 24, 1996. Also Chuck Colson in *In the Lion's Den* by Nina Shea (Nashville: Broadman and Holman Publishers, 1997), ix. "More Christians have been martyred for their faith in this century alone than in the previous nineteen centuries combined."

4. Ibid. Also televised programs of the Christian Broadcasting Company's *700 Club*, including videos of some of the atrocities, Spring 1999.

5. Alister E. McGrath, *Luther's Theology of the Cross* (Grand Rapids: Baker Books, 1985), 171. Bainton, *Here I Stand*, 31, 44–47.

6. *What Luther Says*, 358, #1053; 357, #1049–#1051; 360, #1058.

7. Martin Luther, Sermon at Coburg on "Cross and Suffering" (1530). *LW* 51:202.

8. Soelle, *Suffering*, 171–74.

9. E. Stanley Jones, *Christ and Human Suffering* (New York: Abingdon Press, 1933), 60, 61.

10. Douglas John Hall, *God and Human Suffering: An Exercise in the Theology of the Cross* (Minneapolis, Augsburg, 1987), 80.

11. The first is referred to as *potentia absoluta*, and the second is known as *potentia ordinata*. See McGrath, as below. McGrath discusses "the two powers of God" as used by Aquinas and, particularly, the *via moderna* school. Note: "St. Thomas points out that while God is omnipotent, there are many things which he is perfectly capable of doing, but

which he elects not to do" (55). Also: "God is understood to have imposed upon himself, by a free and uncoerced primordial decision, certain self-limitation, in that he is faithful to the order which he himself has established." "God is unable to construct a triangle with four sides" (56). "Luther . . . does not use the dialectic between the two powers of God to any significant extent, although . . . he incorporates several consequences of its application into his early theology of justification" (58).

12. Elie Wiesel, *Night* (New York: Bantam Edition, 1982), 61, 62.

13. Soelle, *Suffering*, 68–74.

14. Dorothee, Soelle. *Theology for Skeptics* (Minneapolis: Fortress Press, 1995), 15.

9. The Heart Growing in Grace

1. *Common Service Book* (Philadelphia: The Board of Publication of the United Lutheran Church in America, 1917), 237. I have changed *Ghost* to *Spirit*, and *thee* to *you*.

2. Underhill, *Spiritual*, 48.

3. *SBH*, #538.

4. Martin Luther, *Large Catechism, Book of Concord*, trans. and ed. Theodore G. Tappert (Philadelphia: Fortress Press, 1959), 419.

5. Ibid.

6. Martin Luther, *Lectures on Galatians* (1535), *LW* 27:28, 30–31.

7. "Epitome Article II, Free Will," *The Formula of Concord* in *The Book of Concord*, 471. *The Formula of Concord* "represents the definitive statement of Lutheran orthodoxy corresponding to the similar pronouncements. . . of the Council of Trent." From *The Oxford Dictionary of the Christian Church*, ed. F. L. Cross (London: Oxford University Press, 1957), 323.

8. H. George Anderson, *A Good Time to Be the Church* (Minneapolis: Augsburg Fortress, 1997), 30.

9. Ibid., 38. Note that there is much here that can be compared with the Ignatian process of discernment.

10. Luther, "Preface to Romans," 23, 24.

11. Martin Luther, "Two Kinds of Righteousness" in Lull, 158.

12. Luther, "Freedom," 284.

13. Martin Luther, "Two Sermons Preached at Weimar" in *LW* 51:114.

14. Luther, "Lectures on Galatians, 1535," *LW* 26:126.

15. ———, *Defense of All the Articles*, *W* 7:337, 330, trans. William Lazareth, in *Receptive Prayer*, 119.

16. Martin Luther, quoted by Eric Gritsch in Martin, *God's Court Jester: Luther in Retrospect* (Philadelphia: Fortress, 1983), 185.

17. Martin Luther, "Ninety-five Theses," in Lull, 21.

10. The Life-Giving Heart

1. Source unknown to author.

2. Luther, "Freedom," 304.

3. "Sermons on the Gospel of St. John," *LW* 24:143.

4. Theologically this approach is known as "realized eschatology" or experiencing the end times in the present.

5. Rosemary Radford Ruether, in *Western Spirituality: Historical Roots, Ecumenical Routes*, ed. Matthew Fox (Santa Fe: Bear & Company, 1980), p 161.

6. Dorothy Day, quoted in George S. Johnson, *Beyond Guilt and Powerlessness* (Minneapolis: Augsburg, 1983), 26, 27.

7. Underhill, *Ways*, 68.

8. Luther, *Preface to Romans*, *LW* 35:371.

9. Martin Luther, *WA* 5, 169, 12. As quoted in Jared Wicks, S.J., *Luther and His Spiritual Legacy* (Wilmington Del.: Michael Glazier, Inc., 1983), 128.

10. Eckhart, Sermon 3, 115.

11. Ibid., Sermon 7, 135.

12. Martin Buber, *I and Thou* (New York: Charles Scribner's Sons, 1957 edition).

13. Malcolm Muggeridge, *Something Beautiful for God* (San Francisco: Harper & Row, 1971), 73, 74.

14. Ibid., 22.

15. Ibid., 75.

16. Garth Thompson, "Witness Fitness," a sermon, May 16, 1999.

17. Reports from Charles Kernaghan, National Labor Committee, 275 Seventh Avenue, New York, NY 10001. Extremely important reading.

18. Thomas Kelly, *Testament of Devotion*. New York: Harper & Bros., 1941), 109.

19. Marjorie Thompson, *Weavings*, 1:2, 29.

20. Kernaghan. See note 21 also.

21. Interfaith Center on Corporate Responsibility, Tim Smith, Executive Director, 475 Riverside Dr., New York, NY, 10115; Bread for the World, 1100 Wayne Ave., Suite 1000, Silver Spring, MD, 20910; Lutheran Office for Governmental Affairs, c/o Mark Brown, 122 C NW, Suite 125, Washington, D.C., 20001.

22. Mev Puleo, *The Struggle Is One* (Albany: State University of New York Press, 1994).

23. Ibid., p 48. *Conscientization* is a method articulated by the educator Paulo Freire, *Pedagogy of the Oppressed* (New York: Continuum, 1995).

24. Jeff Gates, *The Ownership Solution* (Reading, Mass.: Addison Wesley, 1998).

25. Fox, *Original*, 295, 260.

26. Ibid., 260.

27. Joan D. Chittister, O.S.B., "The Monastic Way," Dec. 1998.

28. Rabindranath Tagore, *Fireflies* (New York: The Macmillan Company, 1928), 205.

29. Martin Luther, *Lectures on Deuteronomy, LW* 9: 96

30. Reuben Job, 22, 23.

31. David L. Miller, "Holy Labor of Love," *Lutheran Women* (March 1999), 7. Also see *Friendship with Jesus* (Minneapolis: Augsburg, 1999), 157, 160–161.

32. Barbara Brown Taylor, *Gospel Medicine* (Cambridge, Mass.: Cowley Publications, 1995), 77, 78.

11. The Committed Heart

1. Martin Luther, A Sermon on Luke 12:35–40, *What Luther Says*, 500, #1495; *W* 17 II:275.

2. "O God, I Love Thee," *SBH*, #489. The original Latin text was

translated by Edward Henry Bickersteth and set to music by John B. Dykes three centuries later.

3. "O Sacred Head, Now Wounded" *LBW*, #117.

4. John Mogabgab, "Editor's Introduction: Commitment," *Weavings*, IX:4, 2.

5. Martin Luther, "Commentary on Psalm 51," *LW* 12:383.

6. Ibid., 384.

7. Fowler, 199–210.

8. Ibid., 200.

9. Catherine Herzel, "Disciples." Source unknown. Catherine Herzel died in May 1999. She wrote at least seven books, the best known of which was written with her husband, Frank, and entitled *To Thee I Sing* (Philadelphia: Muhlenberg Press, 1946).

10. Rollo May, *The Courage to Create* (New York: W. W. Norton & Company, 1975), 17.

11. Robert Coles, ed., "Introduction: The Making of A Disciple," *Dietrich Bonhoeffer* (Maryknoll, N.Y.: Orbis Books, 1998), 40.

12. *What Luther Says*, 361. (Slightly less effectively translated in *LW* 24:197.)

13. Bonhoeffer, *Life Together*, 17.

14. Ibid.

15. Quoted by Henri Nouwen in *Sabbatical Journey* (New York: Crossroad, 1998). Nouwen prayed this prayer daily.

16. Dietrich Bonhoeffer, *The Cost of Discipleship*, trans. R. H. Fuller (New York: The Macmillan Company, 1967 edition; first pub. 1937), 99.

17. Ibid., 51.

18. Foreword by Bishop G. K. A. Bell, "Foreword" in Bonhoeffer, *Cost*.

19. Coles, 19, 20.

20. Ibid., 44.

21. Ibid., 120.

22. Bonhoeffer, *Cost*, 47.

23. Ibid., 63, 64.

24. Coles, 117.

25. Bonhoeffer, *Cost*, 47.

26. Underhill, *Ways*, 73.

27. May, 12.

28. Ibid., p 21.

29. Ibid.

30. Underhill, *Ways*, 158, 159.

31. May, *Courage*, 18, 19.

32. Ibid., 23, 25.

33. William F. Lynch, S.J., *Images of Hope* (Baltimore: Helicon Press, 1965), 129–186.

34. *Julian of Norwich: Showings*, trans. with intro. by Edmund Colledge, O.S.A. and James Walsh, S.J., pref. Jean Leclercq, O.S.B. (New York: Paulist Press, 1978), 149.

35. Paul Tillich, "Yes and No," in *The New Being* (New York: Charles Scribner's Sons, 1955), 103, 104. Also see Paul Tillich, "The Eternal Now" in *The Eternal Now* (New York: Charles Scribner's Sons, 1963), 131.

36. Augustine in *An African Prayer Book* by Desmond Tutu (New York: Doubleday, 1995), 33.

Index of Biblical Passages

INDEX OF NAMES

SUBJECT INDEX

abiding (connectedness to God), 95–109
absence of God, 35, 100
agape, 153
alternative investments, 145
anawim, 145
Anfectung (anxiety), 32, 36, 114
apostles (those sent out), 150–51
attachment, 81–92, 129
authority, 55–58

baptism, 128
base communities, 147–48
belief, 22, 29
belief and trust, 51–64
birth (from God's heart), 27–37
birth of Christ in the heart (*see* Holy Spirit),
    39–47
both/and approach, 12, 89–90

call of God and vocation, 18, 67–79, 82, 101,
    133
capacity for God, 31
capacity to love, 29, 31
choice, 20–21, 33–34, 81–92, 120, 144
commands of God, 21, 29
commitment (consecration, dedication), 18,
    22, 63, 77–79, 153–169
community, 105–106
concientization, 148
confidence in God, 17, 22
contingency, 31
courage, 164–66
covenant, 21, 153, 155
cross/cost of discipleship, 34, 153–169

death, 20, 84, (daily) 131
demythologization, 61–62
detachment, letting go, self-denial, 76, 81–92
devil, 42, 54
Devotio Moderna, en 177

empowerment (giving life, 132–33, 135–51),
    137, 146, 148
estrangement, loneliness (*see* sin), 31–32, 119,
    22
evil, 74, 111–22
experience of God (encounter), 11–12, 42,
    51–64
explanation, 51, 59

faith (five kinds of):
    of the heart (trust, personal knowing, rela-
    tionship), 12

of the head (reason, knowledge about), 12
of the lips (creedal), 12
as way of life (discipline, habits), 12
community of, 12
faith as *fides, fides fiducialis, fiducia,* and *pistis,*
    en 171–72
faith as God's gift, 21, 33
    as seed, 21
faith, as inherited, 55
    as personal, 42, 55–56
    as spirituality, 60
    as transformative, 60
faith, Luther's two kinds:
    historical, 42, 62
    experiential ("faith of the heart"), 42
faithfulness of God, 11, 18–20
fear, 74–75, 92
fideism, 53–54
force by God (control, manipulation, determi-
    nation, intervention), 22, 29, 34–35, 112,
    117, 120–21
forgiveness, 31, 34, 83, 85, 137
freedom, 21, 34, 115, 117 (*see* Luther's *Free-
    dom of A Christian*)

Gelassenheit, 85–86
gifts of the Holy Spirit (Luther's list), 155
giving life, 11, 28, 31, 135–151
God's inviting, enticing, 34
grace, 12, 21, 28, 34, 68, 75, 121–22, cheap-
    163
Great Commandment, the, 21
healing, 18, 85, 119
hearing the Word, 41, 73
heart, 22–23, 27–37, 39–48, 59, 129
history (*see* historical faith):
    God acting in history, 41–42, 118
    historical reality, 62
Holy Spirit (God, Christ within us), 17,
    20–21, 29, 33, 35, 39–47, 42
hope, 166–68
hymn: "I Will Make My Heart A Cradle," 48

integration of theology and spirituality, 13, 14
inside/outside, 40–41, 63, 87, 132

Jubilee Year, 20, 145

kenosis (God's self poured out in love), 28, 67,
    85
kingdom of God, 33, 138
knowing and knowing about God, 11, 32

191